HALLOWEEN
Trivia Book

Welcome to 'Halloween Trivia Facts,' your gateway to the enchanting world of Halloween. Explore 300 curated multiple-choice questions spanning history, fun facts, movies, and more. Whether a casual enthusiast or devoted trivia buff, embark on a journey of discovery. Wishing you a Happy Halloween filled with spooky joy and a deep dive into this captivating book. Happy reading and enjoy the mysteries and delights of the season!

CONTENT

HALLOWEEN TRIVIA : LEVEL EASY

1. What was the original name by which Halloween was called?
a. All Costume Eve
b. After Eve
c. All Hallows' Eve
d. Alter Ego Eve

2. What is typically worn for Halloween?
a. cats
b. costumes
c. carports
d. carnivores

3. Which of the following words describes a malevolent being, generally seeking to do evil?
a. dryad
b. dog
c. demon
d. derby

4. What spooky E word is often used at Halloween?
a. eerie
b. edgy
c. easy
d. envelope

5. What is the name of the malevolent scientist who, with the help of his assistant Igor, brought a monster to life?
a. Frankenweenie
b. Frankenstein
c. Frankenpuss
d. Frank and Alice

6. What is white and filmy and haunts you?
a. garbage
b. gangrene
c. gorilla
d. ghost

7. Where might you encounter ghosts, cobwebs, and portraits that seem to track your every move?
a. haunted houses
b. hotels
c. hospitals
d. hairdresser shops

8. In Washington Irving's Halloween tale "The Legend of Sleepy Hollow," who takes center stage as the main character?
a. Irving Berlin
b. Itchy Scratchalus
c. Inga Bergman
d. Ichabod Crane

9. During Halloween, what do you traditionally transform a pumpkin into?
a. Jack and Jill
b. Jack O'Lantern
c. Jack O'Leary
d. Jack Pumpkin

10. In Disney's "The Adventures of Ichabod and Mr. Toad," which classic novel accompanies "Wind in the Willows" in the storytelling?
a. Legend of Sleepy Hollow
b. Leave it to Ichabod
c. Leaves of Grass
d. Lessons on a Pumpkin

11. Which Tim Burton film combines the themes of Halloween and Christmas?
a. Night Time Santa
b. Night of the Living Dead
c. Nightmare Before Christmas
d. Night Terrors

12. Which orange vegetable is a well-known Halloween symbol, often hollowed out and illuminated with candles inside?
a. parsnip
b. pear
c. peas
d. pumpkin

13. During Halloween, which skeletal beings can be heard making noise in cemeteries?
a. skeletons
b. spaghetti
c. soup bones
d. spiders

14. Which creature feeds on your blood by biting your neck?
a. violinist
b. vixen
c. vampire
d. ventriloquist

15. Among these options, who is not typically associated with spellcasting and magic?

a. witch
b. wiccan
c. warlock
d. weatherman

16. **What Z word is a term for creatures that are animated dead?**
a. zebras
b. zombies
c. zoologists
d. zephyrs

17. **I am a white, billowing figure with eyes and a mouth, often accompanied by the sound of rattling chains. What could I be?**
a. A ghost
b. A witch
c. A cat
d. A goblin

18. **I wear a tall, pointed hat and travel on a broomstick. My appearance might include a green complexion and warts. What identity do I take on?**
a. Zombie
b. Vampire
c. Witch
d. Werewolf

19. **Adorned in a black cape and featuring fangs, my intention is to draw your blood. Who might I be?**
a. Ghost
b. Vampire
c. Zombie
d. Werewolf

20. **With spectacles perched on my nose and a cape flowing, a lightning-shaped scar marks my forehead as I attend Hogwarts School. I'm also keen on soaring through the skies on my broomstick. Who do you think I am?**
a. Professor Snape
b. The Cat in the Hat
c. Harry Potter
d. Sabrina the Teenage Witch

21. **Cloaked in fur and boasting a tail, my appearance is often linked to superstitions in the United States, where a black version of me is thought to bring bad luck. Who am I?**
a. Werewolf
b. Ghost
c. Cat
d. Dog

22. I exclusively emerge under the radiance of the full moon, while for the rest of the month, I appear as an ordinary human. My form is hairy, and I sport both sharp claws and fangs. Who might I be?

a. Vampire
b. Werewolf
c. Ghost
d. Witch

23. As a young student in kindergarten, I team up with my sisters and our extraordinary abilities to frequently rescue the world. Can you guess my identity?

a. Buffy the Vampire Slayer
b. Little Orphan Annie
c. A Powerpuff Girl
d. Sabrina the Teenage Witch

24. Hailing from a renowned horror film, I inquire about my victims' preferred scary movies. Up until 2011, four movies have been released featuring my likeness. What series of movies am I associated with?

a. Halloween
b. Scream
c. Friday the 13th
d. Child's Play

25. I am also a killer from a series of movies. I wear a hockey mask and terrorize counselors at a summer camp. Who am I?

a. Michael
b. Freddie
c. Jason
d. Chucky

26. I might not exude fear, but my teeth certainly do. My vocabulary includes phrases like "groovy baby" and "shagadelic." Adorned in stylish attire, complete with a pendant of the male symbol, I am synonymous with an International Man of Mystery. Who might I be?

a. Scooby Doo
b. Austin Powers
c. Maxwell Smart
d. George W. B ush

27. 'Casper the friendly _____.'

a. Ghost
b. Cat
c. Pumpkin
d. Witch

28. Beware of a _____ cat crossing your path! In the USA, they say it's bad luck.

a. Gray
b. Calico
c. Black
d. Striped

29. Put a light in the _____ to light up its face.
a. Pumpkin
b. Doorway
c. Window
d. Refrigerator

30. Kids love to get _____ when they go "trick or treating"!
a. Fruit
b. Candy
c. Kittens
d. Cereal

31. Witches love to fly around on a _____.
a. Broomstick
b. Dragon
c. Vacuum Cleaner
d. Jet Plane

32. You can dress up in your favorite _____ for Halloween.
a. Barrel
b. Plant
c. Food
d. Costume

33. You can dress up like a _____ on Halloween and wear red horns and a tail.
a. Devil
b. Vegetable
c. Snow Queen
d. Pumpkin

34. To be safe if trick or treating after dark, which of the following should you carry?
a. Bucket
b. Flashlight
c. Cape
d. Cat

35. It's fun, but a little scary to go into the Haunted _____ on Halloween.
a. Lion Cage
b. House
c. Car
d. Waterfall

36. What specific date does Halloween fall on every year?

a. October 13
b. October 1
c. November 1
d. October 31

37. A _____ costume is scary because he wears fangs.
a. Robot
b. Mighty Mouse
c. Vampire
d. Turkey

38. To make a Jack o'Lantern you need to carve a face on a _____.
a. Carrot
b. Squash
c. Birthday Cake
d. Pumpkin

39. A good Halloween game is bobbing for _____.
a. Lemons
b. Do-nuts
c. Playmates
d. Apples

40. Little girls like to put on a crown and dress up like a _____.
a. Princess
b. Clown
c. Frog
d. Witch

41. While it's renowned for creatures like leprechauns and selkies, Halloween is said to have its origins here. Which country are we referring to?
a. France
b. Ireland
c. China
d. Mexico

42. Now, let's journey to Germany, where a curious Halloween tradition involves the discreet placement of knives and sharp objects. What is the underlying purpose for this practice?
a. It's bad luck to cut things
b. To stop ghosts from harming them
c. So children won't hurt themselves
d. To keep their homes neat and tidy

43. Let's go to Mexico, where Halloween is a chance for spirits of departed family members to visit the living. What's the name of this celebration?
a. El Dia de los Gatos
b. El Dia de los Pantalones
c. El Dia de las Trivialidales

d.   El Dia de los Muertos

44.Now in Great Britain, this November 5th holiday isn't on Halloween, but there are still plenty of fireworks and bonfires for this historical figure, whose face graces the masks of both V (from the movie "V for Vendetta") and members of "Anonymous".
a.   David Bowie
b.   Ringo Starr
c.   Guy Fawkes
d.   Martin Luther

45.Japan doesn't celebrate its ghosts and goblins in October. In what summer month is Obon, where the dead are said to return home?
a.   May
b.   December
c.   August
d.   March

46.In what country, where Halloween is known as Alla Helgons Dag, is a national holiday? I wonder if the children there eat my favorite candy fish.
a.   Canada
b.   Argentina
c.   The Netherlands
d.   Sweden

47.In the Czech Republic, it's advisable to arrange some additional chairs on Halloween night. What's the reasoning behind this custom?
a.   For your deceased family members
b.   To have extra seats for your friends
c.   To play musical chairs
d.   All your other chairs will break

48.In Hong Kong, Halloween is known as Yue Lan. What does Yue Lan signify? It's enough to make one's stomach growl just contemplating it.
a.   Festival of the Hungry Ghosts
b.   Festival of the Terrible Ghosts
c.   Festival of the Happy Ghosts
d.   Festival of the Sleepy Ghosts

49.We're close to finishing our spooky tour, but I want to take part in a not-so-scary tradition. If I perform certain rituals and go to sleep on Halloween night, what might I see? This seems more appropriate to February.
a.   My future spouse
b.   My cat
c.   My mother
d.   My worst nightmare

50. **We've returned home, but oh no! A host of ghouls and monsters are trailing behind us! Hurry, what substance can we scatter on the floor to prevent their entry?**
    a. Sprinkles
    b. Salt
    c. Scissors
    d. Cayenne Pepper

51. **As the lights dim and the jack-o'-lanterns emit their eerie glow, the Halloween atmosphere comes alive. What exactly is a jack-o'-lantern?**
    a. A headless horseman
    b. An illuminated device used to change a tire
    c. A lamp used for camping
    d. A carved pumpkin

52. **I turn on the CD player and let the air fill with squeaking, moaning, groaning, creaking and other grotesque sounds. I particularly like to play the song "Thriller". Who sings this?**
    a. Michael Jackson
    b. Michael Landon
    c. Michael Bolton
    d. Michael Douglas

53. **I have a spooky old tree in the yard near the door and have hung some tennis balls covered in white, flowing pieces of cotton. What do these represent?**
    a. Goblins
    b. Vampires
    c. Werewolves
    d. Ghosts

54. **Next to the door I have placed a black cauldron filled with water which is colored red with lots of food coloring. I've created smoke that pours out of the cauldron. What did I use to do this?**
    a. Dry ice
    b. Wood and fire
    c. Baking soda and water
    d. Nitrogen and vinegar

55. **Along my now barren flower garden I have placed some tombstones. Sticking out of the soil near one of the tombstones is a rubber hand. Which television show, from 1964-1966, had a hand named "Thing", which moved around on its own?**
    a. The Munsters
    b. Charmed
    c. Bewitched
    d. The Addams Family

56. I'm almost ready but I do need to get dressed up. I'm going to be a wrinkly old witch. Which of the following would be most useful for make-up, to make me look wrinkly?

    a. Strands of wool
    b. Shoe polish
    c. Eye-brow pencil
    d. Licorice twists

57. My neighbor's little boy is dressing up like a hobo. He has come to ask me for some petroleum jelly and some tea. What is he most probably planning to do with that?

    a. Spike his hair and drink the tea
    b. Shine his shoes
    c. Make a beard
    d. Make his clothes look dirty

58. I was wondering whether or not to invite children into my house, so they could pick out which treat they want. Is it a good idea to go into a stranger's house to do that?

    a. Yes
    b. No

59. I have two cats and a dog. What should I do with them on Halloween night?

    a. Let them greet the children
    b. Put them in a bedroom and close the door
    c. Dress them up and take them out too
    d. Fight with them to keep them from getting outside

60. The evening has been a success, so now that Halloween is over, I settle down to watch a good movie. One of my favorites to watch this time of year stars Goldie Hawn, Meryl Streep and Bruce Willis. What is the name of this 1992 comedy movie directed by Robert Zemeckis?

    a. Edward Scissorhands
    b. Willow
    c. The Labyrinth
    d. Death Becomes Her

61. The practice of wearing costumes on Halloween is believed to have come from which country?

    a. Indonesia
    b. Ireland
    c. Italy
    d. Iran

62. **A being you might see on Halloween is the vampire. Which of the following methods would traditionally be the most effective way to kill a vampire?**
    a. Stake through the heart
    b. Poisoned porridge
    c. With a silver bullet
    d. Have a dog bite him

63. **Which colors are traditionally associated with Halloween?**
    a. Orange and black
    b. Red and white
    c. Blue and gold
    d. Yellow and brown

64. **Eddie Munster was a character on the 1960s television series "The Munsters". Which "Halloween" character does he represent?**
    a. Mummy
    b. Werewolf
    c. Ghost
    d. Vampire

65. **Which name used at Halloween is from an Irish folktale?**
    a. Scaredy Cat
    b. Alfred J. Gross
    c. Jack-O-Lantern
    d. Vampire Valient

66. **Often found in American trick or treat baskets, which of these were the first wrapped penny candy in America?**
    a. Divinity
    b. Jolly Ranchers
    c. Tootsie Rolls
    d. Life Savers

67. **According to traditional beliefs, what was the original name for Halloween?**
    a. Witches Night
    b. Eid ul-Fitr
    c. Blasphemy Day
    d. Samhain

68. **Jack O'Lanterns were originally made from what?**
    a. Turnips
    b. Kholrabi
    c. Watermelon
    d. Beets

69. **Harry Houdini died on Halloween.**
    a. True

b. False

70. The word "witch" comes from the Old English "wicce", meaning "wise woman."
   a. True
   b. False

71. Who is the only one in the gang who believes in the Great Pumpkin?
   a. Charlie Brown
   b. Pigpen
   c. Snoopy
   d. Linus

72. Who kept getting rocks when the gang was out for tricks or treats?
   a. Linus
   b. No one
   c. The Great Pumpkin
   d. Charlie Brown

73. Which kid's identity was given away to the rest of the gang because of the usual cloud of dirt that follows him?
   a. Pigpen
   b. Snoopy
   c. Santa Claus
   d. Linus

74. Snoopy, dressed as a World War I flying ace, imagined that his _____ was an airplane.
   a. dog house
   b. friend
   c. pumpkin
   d. candy

75. Where did almost everyone else go when Linus was waiting in the pumpkin patch for The Great Pumpkin?
   a. to the store
   b. out for tricks or treats
   c. on vacation
   d. home

76. According to Linus, The Great Pumpkin rises up from the most _____ pumpkin patch.
   a. colorful
   b. unscrupulous
   c. sincere
   d. boisterous

77. **Why does Sally wait for the Great Pumpkin with Linus instead of going out for tricks or treats?**
    a. She hates candy
    b. She is in love with him
    c. She has nothing better to do
    d. Linus is her arch-enemy

78. **Who is ashamed to have a brother that believes in the Great Pumpkin?**
    a. Snoopy
    b. Lucy
    c. Linus
    d. Woodstock

79. **Who cuts too many holes in their ghost costume?**
    a. Snoopy
    b. Charlie Brown
    c. The Great Pumpkin
    d. Sally

80. **Who wants Charlie Brown to kick the football in the beginning of the cartoon?**
    a. Woodstock
    b. Sally
    c. Lucy
    d. Snoopy

ANSWERS AND FACTS

1. **All Hallows' Eve**

   All Saints' Day or All Hallows' Day was celebrated on November 1 as the start of the Celtic New Year and beginning of winter. The night before, called All Hallows' Eve, witches and other evil spirits were believed to roam the Earth playing tricks on humans.

2. **costumes**

   Some standard Halloween costumes include ghost, witch, princess, mummy, doctor and clown. Other costumes are based on movies or books, like "Ghostbusters" in the 1980s, and "Harry Potter" in the 2000s.

3. **demon**

   In 1589 a demonologist named Binsfield listed the following major demons and their particular evils: Lucifer (pride), Mammon (avarice), Asmodeus or Ashmodai (lechery), Satan (anger), Beelzebub (gluttony), Leviathan (envy), and Belphegor (sloth).

4. **eerie**

Eerie is defined as: a) inspiring inexplicable fear, dread, or uneasiness; strange and frightening. b) suggestive of the supernatural; mysterious

5. **Frankenstein**

"Frankenstein" is a novel by Mary Shelley. Dr. Frankenstein created a monster who was basically gentle, but was ultimately killed by a frightened mob. Today, many people assume the monster was called Frankenstein.

6. **ghost**

Other words for ghost include the following: apparition, appearance, banshee, eidolon, ethereal being, haunt, incorporeal being, kelpie, manes, phantasm, phantom, poltergeist, revenant, shade, shadow, soul, specter, spirit, and wraith.

7. **haunted houses**

Haunted Houses are prevalent in many Halloween movies and stories. In October, many towns host spook alleys or haunted houses with people dressed up as monsters and scary decorations designed to scare children and adults alike. Haunted mazes are also fun because they are scary and you can get lost.

8. **Ichabod Crane**

Ichabod Crane encounters the legendary local ghost, the Headless Horseman, while leaving the town of Sleepy Hollow on Halloween.

9. **Jack O'Lantern**

Traditional Jack O'Lanterns are carved with faces: eyes, nose, mouth, etc. Also, neat are pumpkins carved with pictures, like a black cat on a picket fence or a witch flying across the moon. You can be very creative when carving pumpkins. Jack-o'-lantern is also the common name for the mushroom species Clitocybe illudens.

10. **Legend of Sleepy Hollow**

"The Legend of Sleepy Hollow" was written by Washington Irving in the 1800s and has been the basis for many movies, including 1999's "Sleepy Hollow" starring Johnny Depp and 1922's "The Headless Horseman" starring Will Rogers.

11. **Nightmare Before Christmas**

This great movie from 1993 is about Jack Skellington, the King of Halloween who accidentally discovers Christmas Town and decides to take over Christmas for that year. This movie features the voice talents of Danny Elfman as the singing voice of Jack Skellington.

12. **pumpkin**

Jack O'Lanterns are a traditional part of Halloween, but many people decorate with uncarved pumpkins and other gourds. Every year Linus (from the "Peanuts" cartoon) spends the night in a pumpkin patch waiting for the "Great Pumpkin" to come and bring him gifts.

13. **skeletons**

A skeleton is defined as "the internal structure composed of bone and cartilage that protects and supports the soft organs, tissues, and other parts of a vertebrate organism, There is something spooky about a creature with no organs, muscles or skin.

14. **vampire**

Vampires are creatures of myth and legend. The most famous is Dracula, the character of a novel by Bram Stoker. Vampires have also become literary characters in Ann Rice's "Interview With a Vampire" (also a 1994 movie starring Tom Cruise, Brad Pitt and Kirsten Dunst).

15. **weatherman**

These terms are defined as follows: Witch: a woman claiming or popularly believed to possess magical powers and practice sorcery.

Warlock: a male witch, sorcerer, wizard, or demon.

Wiccan: a polytheistic Neo-Pagan nature religion inspired by various pre-Christian western European beliefs, whose central deity is a mother goddess and which includes the use of herbal magic and benign witchcraft.

Weatherman: a man who reports and forecasts the weather (no magic involved)

16. **zombies**

Zombies are just one more scary Halloween monster. Some of the greatest are from Michael Jackson's "Thriller" video, where they all start dancing around.

17. **A ghost**

"A ghost is the energy that is freed from the body after death. All things have energy. Those who have a sixth sense can feel their presence and those who realize their existence have a greater chance of seeing them." - The Ohio Ghost Hunters Society

18. **Witch**

Witchcraft means "Craft of the Wise Ones" and is also known as the "Old Religion".

19. **Vampire**

Vampires have been feared in many cultures throughout history. Legend says that Adam's first wife Lilith was a vampire who came back to haunt Adam and Eve.

20. **Harry Potter**

The Harry Potter books are the best selling children's books ever! If you haven't read them, you should. I'm 32, my mother is 59, my niece is twelve and my nephew is five, and we ALL love the Harry Potter books!

21. **Cat**

There are many different superstitions about cats such as if a cat stares out the window it is going to rain, and of course, a cat has nine lives. In ancient Egypt the cat was considered sacred and to kill one was sacrilege. In England black cats are considered lucky!

22. **Werewolf**

The myth of the werewolf dates back mainly to fourteenth-century Europe, although there are earlier references in Greek and Roman literature to men changing into wolves.

23. **A Powerpuff Girl**

The girls were created from Chemical X.

24. **Scream**

The movie "Scream" was released in 1996. It was directed by Wes Craven and written by Kevin Williamson. It featured Neve Campbell, Skeet Ulrich, Courteney Cox and Drew Barrymore.

25. **Jason**

The first movie in the "Friday the 13th" series was released in 1980. In the film, the killer was Mrs. Pamela Voorhees, played by Betsy Palmer, who was angry that camp counselors had allowed her son Jason to drown. In the rest of the films, Jason is the killer.

26. **Austin Powers**

27. **Ghost**

Casper appears in cartoons, comics and movies. He's one of my favorites.

28. **Black**

This is only a superstition, I hope ...

29. **Pumpkin**

The best part of Halloween is carving the pumpkin!

30. **Candy**

Be sure to check out the candy to make sure it's o.k.

31. **Broomstick**

I hope you got this one right, a modern witch might use a plane. (Hee Hee)

32. **Costume**

One of the best parts of Halloween is getting a costume.

33. Devil

I don't see many kids dress up as a devil anymore. I see more super heroes and princesses. I like that!

34. Flashlight

It's always best to be seen for your own safety. Take a flashlight and wear light colored clothes or use reflector tape. Be safe!

35. House

I'm still afraid of Haunted Houses. :-)

36. October 31

Happy Halloween! I hope you got this one right so you don't miss it.

37. Vampire

I like vampire movies but they can be scary sometimes.

38. Pumpkin

In some places squash or turnips can be carved for lanterns. Oh I can't wait for Halloween, this is so much fun!

39. Apples

I never could do this game and it gets your costume wet!

40. Princess

I love to greet the Trick or Treaters, they are so great!

41. Ireland

Originally known as Samhain, an ancient Celtic festival celebrated to ward off ghosts by wearing frightening costumes, Halloween has become a global celebration. Modern Irish Halloween includes eating barnbrack, a raisin bread that has an object inside. Sometimes it's used to tell your fortune!

42. To stop ghosts from harming them

According to Germanic legend, returning spirits will hurt people who leave out anything dangerous.

43. El Dia de los Muertos

El Dia de los Muertos (Day of the Dead) is a popular celebration in Latin America.

Families make beautiful altars for their departed loved ones and celebrate for up to three days. I can only wish for Day of the Cats, Pants, or Trivia!

44. **Guy Fawkes**

Guy Fawkes Night commemorates the arrest of Guy Fawkes, a member of the infamous Gunpowder Plot. Members of the "hacktivist" group Anonymous, which has launched internet attacks on the Church of Scientology and governments among others to protest current events and abuse, have adopted the Guy Fawkes mask while making public statements to keep their identities secret.

45. **August**

In Japan, Obon is celebrated with special foods. Paper boats with candles in them are sent down a river to guide the spirits, and the famous Bon Odori dance is performed. Obon is a traditional (and fun!) summer festival in which all are welcomed to participate.

46. **Sweden**

Not only is Halloween a national holiday, schools have a week of break! Halloween is one of my favorite holidays (and I bet I would have loved it more if I grew up in Sweden!)

47. **For your deceased family members**

The chairs are to remind one of their deceased family members (and to give their ghosts a place to sit, should they visit on Halloween.))

48. **Festival of the Hungry Ghosts**

Even ghosts get hungry on Halloween in Hong Kong! People will burn pictures of fruit or money to feed the ghosts that haunt the streets on Halloween.

49. **My future spouse**

Some older Halloween traditions focused more on future love than a scary past. In several countries, eating sweets, divining the future with egg yolks, or standing in a dark room with a candle and a mirror would show that person's future spouse (who, by legend, would be married to them by next Halloween.)

50. Salt

Salt is a valuable ward against ghosts and monsters in many different cultures, where an unbroken salt barrier will prevent any evil from entering your home.

51. A carved pumpkin

A carved pumpkin is also known as a jack-o'-lantern. To make a jack-o'-lantern you have to remove the top. With a spoon, or even your hands, you can pull out the inner flesh and seeds leaving the inside hollow. With a carving knife a creepy face can be carved from the outside in, right through the pumpkin shell. A glow stick, candle or other source of light is placed inside and the lid is put back on. The jack-o'-lantern will glow, exposing just how creepy the carved face is.

52. Michael Jackson

The Michael Jackson album titled "Thriller" was released in 1982. The single "Thriller" which is on the "Thriller" album lasts four minutes and thirty seven seconds. On the album it lasts longer. It was written by Rod Temperton. Some of the sound effects in this song include thunder, wind, howling, creaking and even feet walking upon some wooden planks.

The music video, which is called "Michael Jackson's Thriller" (1983), lasts fourteen minutes.

53. Ghosts

A good way to create ghosts to hang from a tree is to get some tennis or Styrofoam balls and cover them with pieces of old white cotton sheets. You can paint on some eyes and mouths with a black marker to give the ghosts some form of identity. Fishing line is quite clear so it works well to tie the ghosts onto tree branches. The ghosts really look like they are floating.

54. Dry ice

Dry ice is carbon dioxide in the form of a solid, and is also sometimes called "Cardice" and "card ice". Typically, it is used to keep food frozen or preserved with the use of non-cyclic refrigeration, and is also used in the making of ice cream. To create the smoke, all one has to do is place the dry ice into water - but be very careful not to touch the dry ice, use tongs instead. Sublimation happens when dry ice mixes into water, which makes the fog or smoke effect. Sublimation is when a solid changes into a gas without becoming a liquid in between.

55. The Addams Family

Thing T. Thing was the full name of the right hand, in "The Addams Family" (1964-1966) television show. Thing was also in "The New Addams Family" (1998) as well as the more recent movies. Thing's duties in the television show included getting the mail, giving Gomez some cigars and lighting them. Thing also would be seen helping Morticia by holding her wool when she was knitting.
When the Addams family would go for a drive, Thing would go along as well and ride in the glove compartment.

56. Eye-brow pencil

Eye-brow pencil works really well to make wrinkles. I smile really big and squint at the same time. When I see which lines on my face could become a wrinkle, when I actually do get old, I draw them onto my skin with my eye-brow pencil. When I am done, I really look wrinkly and old. I draw on a couple of smudges to look like black warts on my nose and my chin. I have long hair, so before I put on my pointy hat I comb my hair backwards so it is all frizzy and knotted looking. It is a perfect messy look for a witch!

57. Make a beard

He is going to create the look of a beard on his face. It's easy. You just have to put a thin layer of petroleum jelly on your face, where a beard would be. Once you do that, you break open the tea bag and stick bits of tea onto the petroleum jelly. It will look like whiskers.

58. No

It is never a good idea to enter a stranger's house, even though it is Halloween. If you are invited indoors, just say no thank you and continue on your way. Another bit of advice is that you should not go "trick or treating" alone.

59. Put them in a bedroom and close the door

If you have pets it is a very good idea to put them into a bedroom, with food and water, maybe even a litter box, and close the door. Leave them in that room until Halloween is finished. With so many children and parents walking around, door to door, it can frighten your animals.

They could scratch or bite by accident. Some of them could even run away because they are frightened. To protect them and keep them safe, it is really best to put them where they won't escape outdoors, unnoticed and possibly get lost.

60. Death Becomes Her

"Death Becomes Her" (1992) is a comedy about a writer named Helen (Goldie Hawn) and an actress named Madeline (Meryl Streep) who despise one another. Madeline and Ernest (Bruce Willis) are married, but Ernest used to be Helen's fiance. Helen plots to try to get Ernest back and murder Madeline. One thing leads to another and both women drink a potion that will make them immortal.

They both get killed and become revived as "undead", forcing them to have to maintain their decomposing bodies for all eternity.

61. Ireland

In Ireland, dressing up during this time of the year was common. It was believed that the practice hid the identity of the participant. It became popular for children to wear costumes and "trick or treat" at the beginning of the 20th century.

62. Stake through the heart

To kill a vampire you must drive a stake through its heart. Vampires originated in Europe and were originally believed to be real.

63. Orange and black

Orange was a symbol of strength and endurance and stands for the harvest and autumn. Black was typically a symbol of death and darkness. It also acted as a reminder that Halloween celebrated the boundaries between life and death.

64. Werewolf

Eddie Munster was played by actor Butch Patrick. Eddie was a werewolf boy, and slept in either a coffin or a bureau drawer. His costume consisted of a widow's peak, pointed ears, and fangs. "The Munsters" television series first aired on September 24th, 1964 and ran until May 12th, 1966.

65. Jack-O-Lantern

The name Jack-O-Lantern first originated from an Irish folktale about a man named Stingy Jack who tricked the Devil over and over again. When Jack died, he was forced to walk the Earth with only a carved-out turnip and burning coal to help light his way.

66. Tootsie Rolls

Tootsie rolls were the first wrapped penny candy in America. They are very popular and are given out commonly at Halloween.

67. Samhain

Samhain is a Gaelic festival marking the beginning of the dark part of the year. It occurred between the autumn equinox and the winter solstice. Dances and bonfires were used during the celebration.

68. Turnips

Jack O'Lanterns were originally made from turnips. Jack O'Lanterns were meant to frighten away evil spirits. When pumpkins were discovered, they were found to be much easier to carve, thus the transition.

69. True

Harry Houdini was one of the most famous and mysterious magicians to ever have lived. Strangely, he died in 1926 on Halloween night as a result of appendicitis brought on by three stomach punches.

70. True

Wicce were very respected people at one time. According to popular belief, witches held one of their two main meetings, also known as sabbats, on Halloween night.

71. Linus

Linus is the only one in the gang who believes in the Great Pumpkin in the classic Halloween special, It's the Great Pumpkin, Charlie Brown. Interestingly, the character of Linus was inspired by Charles Schulz's own son, who also carried a security blanket and believed in the existence of the Great Pumpkin.

The Great Pumpkin has become a pop culture icon and is often referenced in other TV shows and movies. In fact, a Great Pumpkin-themed amusement park attraction was created in Japan in 2016.

72. Charlie Brown

In "It's the Great Pumpkin, Charlie Brown," poor Charlie Brown keeps getting rocks instead of candy while out trick-or-treating with his friends. This classic Halloween special first aired in 1966 and has been a beloved tradition for many families ever since.

Interestingly, the voice of Charlie Brown was actually provided by a child actor named Peter Robbins, who was just 9 years old at the time of recording. Despite its initial mixed reviews, the special has become a cultural phenomenon and is still enjoyed by audiences of all ages every Halloween season.

73. Pigpen

Pigpen, the character from It's the Great Pumpkin, Charlie Brown, is known for his perpetually dirty appearance and the cloud of dust that follows him wherever he goes. Interestingly, the character was never actually referred to as "Pigpen" in the original comic strip, but rather as "Pig-Pen" with a hyphen.

The character's design was based on Charles Schulz's own son, who was known for his messy appearance. Despite his uncleanliness, Pigpen is a beloved character in the Peanuts universe and is often seen as a symbol of individuality and self-acceptance.

74. dog house

Snoopy's dog house is an iconic symbol in the Peanuts comic strip and has been featured in various adaptations, including the Halloween special, It's the Great Pumpkin, Charlie Brown. In the special, Snoopy imagines himself as a World War I flying ace and uses his dog house as a makeshift airplane to engage in aerial battles with the Red Baron.

The image of Snoopy atop his dog house, wearing his aviator hat and goggles, has become a beloved and recognizable image in popular culture.

75. **out for tricks or treats**

While waiting in the pumpkin patch for The Great Pumpkin, Linus was left alone as almost everyone else went out for tricks or treats. Halloween is a holiday celebrated in many countries around the world, with traditions varying from region to region. In the United States, trick-or-treating is a popular Halloween tradition where children dress up in costumes and go door-to-door asking for candy.

However, in some countries like Mexico, they celebrate Dia de los Muertos (Day of the Dead) where they honor their deceased loved ones with colorful altars and offerings.

76. **sincere**

Linus believes that The Great Pumpkin will rise up from the most sincere pumpkin patch. This belief is a recurring theme in the classic Halloween special, "It's the Great Pumpkin, Charlie Brown." Interestingly, the special was originally met with mixed reviews and was even criticized for being too slow-paced and melancholic for a children's program.

However, over time, it has become a beloved holiday tradition for many families and is often cited as one of the greatest Halloween specials of all time.

77. **She is in love with him**

Sally's decision to wait for the Great Pumpkin with Linus instead of going out for tricks or treats is not due to her love for him. In fact, in the TV special "It's the Great Pumpkin, Charlie Brown," Sally is shown to have a crush on Linus, but her decision to wait with him is because she believes in the Great Pumpkin just as much as he does. Sally is convinced that the Great Pumpkin will rise from the pumpkin patch and bring toys to all the good little children.

This belief is what leads her to wait with Linus, despite missing out on the Halloween festivities.

78. Lucy

Lucy is the character from "It's the Great Pumpkin, Charlie Brown" who is ashamed to have a brother that believes in the Great Pumpkin. Interestingly, "It's the Great Pumpkin, Charlie Brown" was the third Peanuts special to air on television, following "A Charlie Brown Christmas" and "Charlie Brown's All-Stars." The special originally aired on October 27, 1966, and has since become a Halloween classic.

The Great Pumpkin has also become a pop culture icon, with references to it appearing in various TV shows and movies.

79. Charlie Brown

Charlie Brown is a beloved character from the comic strip Peanuts, created by Charles M. Schulz. In the Halloween special, It's the Great Pumpkin, Charlie Brown, Charlie Brown decides to dress up as a ghost, but he cuts too many holes in his costume, resulting in a less-than-scary appearance.

The special first aired in 1966 and has since become a Halloween classic, with viewers eagerly anticipating the annual broadcast. Despite Charlie Brown's costume mishap, the special teaches valuable lessons about friendship, perseverance, and the importance of believing in something, even if others don't understand or support it.

80. Lucy

Lucy is the character in the Peanuts gang who always holds the football for Charlie Brown to kick, only to pull it away at the last second, causing Charlie Brown to fall. This running gag has been a staple of the Peanuts comic strip and animated specials for decades.

Interestingly, the voice of Lucy was originally performed by a male actor, and it wasn't until later adaptations that a female actress was cast in the role.

HALLOWEEN TRIVIA : LEVEL AVERAGE

81. What coulrophobic phenomenon allegedly occurred in the weeks leading up to Halloween 2016?

a. Bin Laden sightings
b. Mothman sightings
c. Elvis sightings
d. Clown sightings

82. **The ghosts of Al Capone, Birdman Stroud, and other notorious notables are said to haunt what former federal penitentiary?**
   a. Leavenworth
   b. Sing-Sing
   c. Alcatraz
   d. Andersonville

83. **MOVIES / HORROR: Which of these statements about the terrifying classic "Halloween" of 1978 and the subsequent "Halloween" of 2018 is NOT true?**
   a. Both star Jamie Lee Curtis
   b. The killer Michael Myers appears in both
   c. Both are scored by John Carpenter
   d. The 2018 movie is a reboot of the 1978 movie

84. **U.S. HISTORY: Who was the first person executed in the Salem witch trials of colonial Massachusetts?**
   a. Abigail Adams
   b. Virginia Dare
   c. Mary Walcott
   d. Bridget Bishop

85. **LITERATURE / POETRY: A poem traditionally recited at Halloween is "Halloween" (1785), a mixture of Scots and English written by what poet known as the Bard of Ayshire?**
   a. Robert Burns
   b. Samuel Coleridge Taylor
   c. Lord Byron
   d. William Blake

86. **CELEBRITIES: Three of these four celebrities were born on Halloween (October 31). Who is the odd one out?**
   a. John Candy
   b. Ron Kovic
   c. Peter Jackson
   d. Rob Schneider

87. **GEOGRAPHY / CANADA: According to local legend, the first known mention of trick-or-treating in North America occurred in what Canadian province known for Rocky Mountain foothills, the Yellowhead Pass, fertile plains, herds of beef cattle, and the Athabasca Oil Sands?**
   a. Alberta
   b. Newfoundland and Labrador

    c.   Prince Edward Island
    d.   Ontario

88. HUMANITIES / MYTHOLOGY & LEGEND: Halloween was influenced by an ancient Roman festival that celebrated what wood nymph, keeper of apple trees, and goddess of fruitful abundance?
    a.   Juno
    b.   Minerva
    c.   Pomona
    d.   Clio

89. SCIENCE / ASTRONOMY: A full moon that appears in October in the Northern Hemisphere is typically known in American folklore as a Hunter's Moon, or what other more Halloween-y name that has come also to mean a total lunar eclipse?
    a.   Beaver Moon
    b.   Blood Moon
    c.   Hunger Moon
    d.   Frost Moon

90. ANIMALS / CATS: Black cats have been believed in some cultures to be witches' familiars. What chemical makes a cat's fur appear solid black?
    a.   albumin
    b.   sysadmin
    c.   cyanocobalamin
    d.   melanin

91. What did the Celts originally call the festival we now know as Halloween?
    a.   All Hollow's Eve
    b.   Halloween
    c.   Octoberrest
    d.   Samhain

92. In which century did the Catholic Church start to honor the various saints who didn't have their own day already on the calendar, by acknowledging them on November 1, All Hallow's Day, also known as "All Saints' Day"?
    a.   Fourth Century
    b.   Eighth century
    c.   Sixth Century
    d.   Ninth Century

93. What is the traditional dish eaten in Ireland on Halloween?
    a.   Corned Beef and Cabbage
    b.   Colcannon
    c.   Bangers and Mash
    d.   Elvers and Chips

94. **What is the traditional cake eaten in Ireland on Halloween?**
    a. Pumpkin Pie
    b. Carrot Cake
    c. Bracken Pie
    d. Barmbrack Cake

95. **What vegetable was originally used in Ireland to hold the light, before pumpkins became more popular?**
    a. Rutabagas
    b. Turnips
    c. Acorn Squashes
    d. Cabbages

96. **The Celts wore costumes on their Samhain, too. What did the costumes that they wore depict?**
    a. Spirits and devils
    b. Lambs and lions
    c. Angels and archangels
    d. Donkeys and pigs

97. **One of the most popular games at an Irish Halloween party is trying, while blindfolded, to get a bite of a piece of food that's hanging on a string from the ceiling. The first one to get a decent bite out of it gets to keep it, and eat it all. What is the food hanging from the ceiling?**
    a. Pear
    b. Malteaser
    c. Lamb shank
    d. Apple

98. **Halloween is always better if one can have an outdoor bonfire. However, many of us don't have the proper places to do so, so we'll use a fireplace instead. What does Irish tradition require you put in the embers of the fire?**
    a. A cutting of fingernail
    b. A piece of hair
    c. A dried wart
    d. A wing of a bat

99. **Fairies and goblins try to collect as many people on Halloween as they can, so (according to Irish tradition) what should you do if you see one in order to protect yourself as well as to help others?**
    a. Spit over your right shoulder
    b. Snap your right fingers
    c. Throw salt over your left shoulder
    d. Throw dust at them

100. **It's late, so there is just one thing left for Irish people to do this Halloween and that is to check on their animals to ensure that they are in**

**good health. What would you do to them if you saw one that didn't look
very well?**

    a.   Throw dust on him

    b.   Spit on him

    c.   Take him to the emergency veterinary clinic

    d.   Put him out of his misery

101.   **The Halloween tradition is generally thought to be connected to the
Celtic festival of Samhain. The ancient Celts believed that during this time
the border to the Otherworld became thin, allowing spirits to pass
through. Costumes and masks were used to ward off the evil spirits. In its
original Old Irish form, what does Samhain translate to?**

    a.   Summer's end

    b.   Devil's playground

    c.   Celtic New Year

    d.   All Hallows Eve

102.   **In addition to trick or treating, children in the USA sometimes
collect small-change donations for a particular children's charity. What is
the name of this charity which helps the needy children of the world?**

    a.   Sun Youth

    b.   Red Cross

    c.   UNICEF

    d.   Amnesty International

103.   **The tradition of carving out pumpkins to create jack-o'-lanterns has
long been a mainstay of the Halloween festivities. In the past, however,
during Celtic festivals another vegetable was used instead. Which
vegetable was this?**

    a.   Squash

    b.   Turnip

    c.   Eggplant

    d.   Cabbage

104.   **The original "Halloween" movie was released in 1978. The plot is
centered around Michael Myers as he stalks and kills teenage babysitters
on Halloween night. Which actress played the role of the babysitter,
Laurie Strode?**

    a.   Lorraine Bracco

    b.   Ellen Barkin

    c.   Jamie Lee Curtis

    d.   Linda Blair

105.   **In some regions of the world Halloween is held for an extended
period of time. Catholics in Austria and Southern Germany traditionally
celebrate from October 30th to November 8th. What is Halloween called
in those countries?**

a. Frankfurter
b. Austerlitz
c. Seelenwoche
d. Spreckels

106.   Playing with the Ouija Board is particularly popular during Halloween as contact with the afterlife is believed by some to be more likely. Which corporation currently markets the modern Ouija Board?

a. Mayfair Games
b. Mattel
c. Hasbro
d. Milton Bradley

107.   There are a number of poems that are traditionally recited at Halloween. One such poem is called "The Witches' Spell", which takes the form of an extract from a famous Shakespeare play. Which play is it?

a. Hamlet
b. Macbeth
c. King Lear
d. Othello

108.   There have been many songs that have become associated with Halloween through the years. One that comes to mind is a particular Michael Jackson song and video that in its full version lasted 14 minutes. Which one of his masterpieces was this?

a. Thriller
b. Beat It
c. Billie Jean
d. Pretty Young Thing

109.   Many people consider Halloween to be a very scary time of the year, although the majority of people can handle this fear in a rational way. Some, however, cannot. What phobia is associated with Halloween?

a. Hallowphobia
b. Samhainophobia
c. Spookaphobia
d. Triskaidekaphobia

110.   Michael Landon, Dan Rather, Sally Kirkland and Peter Jackson were celebrities all born on Halloween in different years. Who in this group was born first?

a. Michael Landon
b. Peter Jackson
c. Sally Kirkland
d. Dan Rather

111.   According to legend, how do you kill a vampire?

a. Cremate it

b. Bury it at a crossroads
c. Pound a stake through its heart
d. All of these

112. The word Halloween derives from which of the following?
a. All Hallow's Eve
b. Samhain
c. All Saints Day
d. Nothing, it's always been Halloween

113. Which 1993 movie feature characters such as Max, Dani, and Allison?
a. Hocus Pocus
b. Halloween
c. Halloweentown
d. The Witches of Eastwick

114. Which of these animals is considered a bad omen around Halloween?
a. Bat
b. Cockroach
c. Dog
d. Mouse

115. Which of these sings "Monster Mash"?
a. Dr. Demento
b. Bobby Pickett
c. Billy Ray Cyrus
d. Frankie Avalon

116. What phase of moon supposedly makes people act crazier and causes humans to turn into werewolves?
a. Harvest moon
b. Quarter moon
c. Full moon
d. Half moon

117. Several objects are baked into a Barmbrack cake, which is eaten in Ireland on Halloween. This includes a piece of rag. What does that signify if it appears in your slice?
a. Your financial outlook looks gloomy
b. You will get a new outfit
c. Your hats need replacing
d. You will lose your wallet

118. Which cabbage dish is eaten for dinner by Irish families during Halloween?
a. Coleslaw

b. Colcannon

c. Kapuska

d. Dim Sims

119. The carving of pumpkins in Ireland during Halloween is said to have started by an Irish blacksmith who carried out which sin?

a. Colluding with Old Nick

b. Murdering his seven wives

c. Stealing horses

d. Stealing potatoes

120. The Ancient Celts of Ireland first celebrated Halloween as which pagan festival?

a. Beltane

b. Samhain

c. Imbolc

d. Lughnasadh

121. Which other popular Halloween tradition is also believed to have originated in Ireland?

a. Bobbing for apples

b. Dressing up in costumes

c. Throwing eggs at cars

d. Decorating gardens with toilet paper

122. The Ivy Leaf is another interesting Irish Halloween tradition. One is plucked and then left overnight in which simple container?

a. A garden hose

b. A family tomb

c. A cup of water

d. A washing tub

123. Snap Apple is a children's game played in Ireland during Halloween. Where is the apple placed?

a. Suspended from a piece of string overhead

b. In the bedroom of a grandmother

c. Hidden in a barn

d. Under the kitchen table

124. Souls must be protected from fairies and goblins during an Irish Halloween. How is this done?

a. Dancing a jig backwards

b. Praying

c. Throwing the dust under your feet at them

d. Eating raw potatoes

125. **What do single romantic Irish lads and lasses drop into bonfires during Halloween celebrations?**
    a. A lock of their hair
    b. Orange peels
    c. Cut fingernails
    d. Broken harps

126. **Another way to find one's true love during an Irish Halloween is, somewhat peculiarly, carrying out which green thumb activity?**
    a. Uprooting a cabbage
    b. Peeling onions
    c. Chopping down a cherry tree
    d. Chasing a horse

127. **I heard some talk around the castle that some of our customs during Allhallowtide are "too pagan". When I asked My Lady, the Countess of Warwick, she assured me that our observances are in accordance with the Church. She also said, however, that some Allhallowtide customs are reminiscent of which Celtic festival?**
    a. Beltaine
    b. Imbolc
    c. Yule
    d. Samhain

128. **During Allhallowtide we carve vegetables, which are used as lanterns. Which vegetable do we commonly use?**
    a. Kale
    b. Potato
    c. Turnip
    d. Beet

129. **One of our customs during Allhallowtide is to "go souling". What is received by those who participate in this activity?**
    a. Special Blessings
    b. Soul Cakes
    c. Costumes
    d. Coins

130. **Fortune telling is a popular activity during Allhallowtide on the manor of My Lord, the Earl of Warwick. Which of the following is a popular way to learn one's future in mediaeval England?**
    a. Follow a divining rod
    b. Look into a crystal ball
    c. Pouring egg whites into hot water
    d. Read palms

131. **My Lady told us an interesting story about the Roman goddess Pomona. In all probability, the Romans introduced this custom to**

England and is the reason why we bob for which fruit during Allhallowtide?
- a. Plums
- b. Pears
- c. Apples
- d. Tomatoes

132. **My Lady reminded all of us pages that we need to prepare some sort of costume to wear during Allhallowtide. Why do we do this?**
- a. So we can play tricks on each other anonymously
- b. So that everyone at the celebration is equal
- c. There is always a contest to see who has the best costume
- d. So the spirits will not recognize us

133. **Our Allhallowtide begins at nightfall on October 31. Which holy day is observed on November 1?**
- a. The Feast of the Immaculate Conception
- b. Feast of the Assumption
- c. Ascension Thursday
- d. All Saints Day

134. **My Lady, the Countess of Warwick, also reminded us pages that we need to collect firewood for the bonfire on All Hallow's Eve. She said the ancient Celts believed that the reason for the fire was to keep the devil at bay.**
- a. True
- b. False

135. **One of the traditions on the manor of My Lord, the Earl of Warwick, is that the priest will lead us to the cemetery one of the nights during Allhallowtide. What will we pour on the graves?**
- a. Honey
- b. Blood
- c. Milk
- d. Wine

136. **The final day of our Allhallowtide observance is called All Soul's Day. How will we commemorate this day?**
- a. Watching a passion play
- b. Dancing
- c. Waging war
- d. Praying for dead Christians

137. **Your first trick or treater is a little boy, dressed in a space suit that has a badge reading 'Space Ranger' and a light green belt. Who is this space man?**
- a. Luke Skywalker
- b. Jimmy Neutron

    c.   Invader Zim
    d.   Buzz Lightyear

138.   **Oh how refreshing! The next little girl is wearing a classic character's costume. She has a pretty dress that is blue and red on the top, and yellow on the bottom, she is wearing a red ribbon in her dark hair. Do you know who she is?**
    a.   Sleeping Beauty
    b.   Cinderella
    c.   Snow White
    d.   Belle

139.   **Luckily the little boy in green's mother shows up minutes later and they continue on their way. As they are leaving two little kids approach. One is dressed in a blue fuzzy costume with big round eyes and looks hungry. The other is in a green fuzzy costume with big round eyes, and he looks grumpy. Who are these fuzzy characters?**
    a.   Grover and Herry
    b.   Cookie Monster and Oscar
    c.   Cookie Monster and Elmo
    d.   Elmo and Oscar

140.   **As you check your candy supply a little girl rings the doorbell. She has long blonde hair and is wearing a light blue dress with a white apron type thing over it. Who is she?**
    a.   Little Orphan Annie
    b.   Little Red Riding Hood
    c.   Alice (in Wonderland)
    d.   Ariel

141.   **After calling the police on a man dressed in all red and holding a sign that reads 'Tickle Me' you greet your next trick or treater. He is wearing a brown dog costume and has a yellow and blue collar tag with initials on it. Who is this doggy?**
    a.   Snoopy
    b.   Blue
    c.   Clifford
    d.   Scooby Doo

142.   **After handing out canned food, money and some of your spouse's cds, you resort to hiding. You turn out the lights just as a little boy in a black mask and a black cape is walking up your sidewalk. Phew. He walks away. It's okay, he was a bad guy anyway. Who was that masked child?**
    a.   Mickey Mouse
    b.   Batman

    c.   Darth Vader

    d.   A power ranger

143.   **The familiar Jack o' Lanterns are thought to have originated in which country?**

    a.   United States

    b.   Spain

    c.   Ireland

    d.   Egypt

144.   **What is the meaning of the word "hallow" in relation to this holiday?**

    a.   Saint

    b.   Candy

    c.   Witch

    d.   Winter

145.   **A popular Halloween candy in the USA, what was the first penny candy to be individually wrapped for sale?**

    a.   Tootsie Rolls

    b.   Peppermint sticks

    c.   Hershey Kisses

    d.   Bit-O-Honey

146.   **The ancient Celts believed that evil spirits were roving the countryside on Halloween night. What did they do in an attempt to protect themselves?**

    a.   They burned candy a fruit in a bonfire

    b.   They bobbed for apples

    c.   They wore masks and costumes

    d.   They went door to door giving their neighbors treats

147.   **All of these celebrities were born on Halloween except one; can you tell me which one does not belong?**

    a.   Michael Landon

    b.   Dan Rather

    c.   John Candy

    d.   River Phoenix

148.   **There is an old belief that it is good luck to see which of the following on Halloween?**

    a.   Bat

    b.   Black Cat

    c.   Spider

    d.   Pumpkin

149.   **The "Monster Mash", often played around the Halloween holiday, was a 1962 novelty song by which of the following groups?**

    a.   "Sir" Jack O'Lantern and the Pumpkin Smashers

b. David "Doctor" Livingstone and the Tomb-Raiders
c. Bobby "Boris" Pickett and the Crypt-Kickers
d. "Lord" Paul Bearer and the Grave-Diggers

150.   What was the point of the old Scottish Halloween tradition involving a young woman peeling an apple in one long strip and then throwing it over her shoulder?

a. The peel was believed to land in the shape of the first letter of the future spouse
b. It would land in the shape of the number of children she would have
c. It would protect you against miscarriage
d. It would protect you from the plague

151.   If you are afraid of Halloween, it might be said that you suffer from which of the following?

a. Pumpkinophobia
b. Samhainophobia
c. Chemophobia
d. Aquaphobia

152.   There are pumpkins that are blue instead of orange.

a. True
b. False

153.   According to some beliefs, what was the original name for Halloween?

a. Tuesday
b. The Devil's Night
c. Samhain
d. Satan's Night

154.   What animal other than a cat is sometimes associated with Halloween?

a. bird
b. dog
c. bat
d. snake

155.   Where did the witch trials of New England take place?

a. Boston, MA
b. Salem, MA
c. Augusta, ME
d. Providence, RI

156.   What country are mummies most associated with?

a. Australia
b. Japan
c. Italy
d. Egypt

157. How do you kill a vampire?
a. Garlic
b. A cross
c. A kiss
d. Stake through the heart

158. When can werewolves come out?
a. Halloween Night
b. During a full moon
c. Dark Nights
d. when a child dies

159. Why do zombies often wear chains?
a. the devil owns them
b. they are slaves
c. they never wear chains
d. they keep them from becoming human

160. On which continent did the stories of vampires originate?
a. Europe
b. Africa
c. Asia
d. America

ANSWERS AND FACTS

81. Clown sightings

Beginning in August 2016 in the USA and around the world, people began reporting sightings of "evil clowns" near woodlands, settings, and other incongruous settings. Many of these were hoaxes or pranks, and the reports began to drain the resources of law enforcement.

The phenomenon was spread mostly as mass hysteria through viral videos (many of which were fake) and social media. Hundreds of students at Penn State university formed a posse to hunt a clown allegedly spotted on campus. Shops from Ohio to New Zealand removed clown costumes from their shelves, and many schools and communities banned clown costumes as well.

There were rumors of a widespread "clown purge" to take place on Halloween that year. While nothing occurred on a large scale, in Orange County, California, a family was attacked by a group of twenty hoodlums in clown mask on October 31,

2016.

The crime remains unsolved.

82. Alcatraz

Alcatraz is an island off the coast of California that once housed a military fort and then a prison, now a tourist attraction. From the beginning, Alcatraz had eerie and punitive associations. Native Americans believed the island to be inhabited by evil spirits, and would banish offenders there, sometimes for life.

There were reports of unexplained noises and visions even while Alcatraz was still in a prison. Some claim to hear in Cellblock B the sound of infamous gangster Al Capone strumming a banjo (although he was never permitted a musical instrument). Full-bodied apparitions of murderer Robert "Birdman" Stroud are claimed to appear in the double cell in which Stroud lived for eleven years in solitary confinement. (He was allowed birds at Leavenworth, hence his nickname, but in Alcatraz this privilege was denied him, and so he haunts in revenge, or so the legend goes.)

83. The 2018 movie is a reboot of the 1978 movie

The "Halloween" slasher franchise centers on an insane villain named Michael Myers who repeatedly escapes and goes on murderous rampages. "Halloween" (2018) is not a reboot of "Halloween" (1978) but meant to be a direct continuation, retconning all the films that came in between (in other words, it more or less ignores them). The heroine in both films is scream queen Jamie Lee Curtis as Laurie Strode, a traumatized babysitter in 1978 and a PTSD-suffering divorced mother in 2018, and in both cases the sister of the vengeful Myers. John Carpenter wrote the musical score for both films and directed the original film, which he co-wrote with Debra Hill.

At the time "Halloween" (2018) premiered, it proved to be the biggest horror movie opening with a female lead, and the biggest opening of any Hollywood movie with a female lead over 55.

84. Bridget Bishop

Bridget Bishop has attracted speculation about her character and behavior over time.

According to folklore, she was a buxom and boisterous and entertaining tavern-keeper, given to showy costumes for a Puritan (a red bodice!), full of gossip and spirit. By the 21st century, however, it was clear that she had been conflated with tavern-keeper Sarah Bishop. Bridget Bishop was a widow (and formerly a battered wife) whose husband had left no will, and is a classic case of a vulnerable, propertied woman being accused of witchcraft. Not understanding that confession was the only way to escape execution, she insisted upon her innocence in court. She was hanged in 1692 and her property confiscated.

In total, nine women and five men were executed in the USA's deadliest witch hunt, "the rock," according to historian G.L. Burr, "on which [colonial] theocracy shattered."

85. Robert Burns

Robert Burns (1759-1796) may be the national poet of Scotland, but he nearly moved to Jamaica; that is, until his "Poems, Chiefly in the Scottish Dialect" began to take off. In that best-selling volume was "Halloween", which at 28 stanzas is one of Burns' longer poems, full of bogies (ghosts), fairies, and mischief.

Its combination of Scots and English with vivid imagery made it a holiday favorite among some of his rural countrymen. "Upon that night, when fairies light..."

86. Ron Kovic

Ron Kovic -- Vietnam vet, author, and anti-war activist -- was the subject of Oliver Stone's "Born on the Fourth of July" (1988), so named for his birthday.

A 2011 study from Yale concluded that 5% fewer babies are born on Halloween than any other day of the year (leap years included). Peter Jackson (b. 1961) directed the "Lord of the Rings" trilogy. Rob Schneider (b. 1963) made his fame on "Saturday Night Live" and in the "Ace Ventura" movies. John Candy (1950-1990) got his start on "Second City Television" and was known for "Uncle Buck" and many more movies.

Also born on Halloween:

- Willow Smith (b. 2000), diva daughter of actors Will Smith and Jada Pinkett-

Smith;

- Astronaut Michael Collins (b. 1930), who stayed in the command module whilst Neil Armstrong and Buzz Aldrin walked on the moon;

- Romantic poet John Keats (1795-1821), who wrote "Ode to a Nightingale" among other classics

87. Alberta

With undulating grasslands, Alberta is Canada's largest producer of beef. The Athabasca oil sands are huge deposits of bitumen (heavy crude oil) that first came to the attention of fur-traders in 1719. They are named after the Athabasca River which cuts through the heart of the deposit, and the Cree and Dene Aboriginal peoples once used the bitumen that washed ashore on its banks to waterproof their canoes. Jasper National Park contains the Yellowhead Pass which crosses the Continental Divide in the Canadian Rockies on the border between Alberta and British Colombia. Hudson's Bay Company used the Pass in the 1820s-50s to transport leather to trappers in New Caledonia (now central British Columbia).

88. Pomona

Pomona was an early deity among the "numina", one of the guardian spirits who were not originally depicted in human form. She was also was the caretaker of gardens and orchards. Her name comes from the Latin word pomum, "fruit," from which many languages derive their word for apple (such as "pomme" in French). Though commonly associated with the Greek goddess Demeter, Pomona really has no Greek counterpart.

She is usually depicted with a cornucopia, and there sits a bronze statue of Pomona atop the Pulitzer Fountain in Manhattan, New York.

The apple-bobbing and nut-cracking customs of Halloween arose from the Pomona festival; indeed some older names for Halloween are Snap-Apple Night and Nutcrack Night.

89. Blood Moon

The Harvest Moon is the first full moon nearest the autumnal equinox, and the

Hunter's Moon appears afterward. Usually the Harvest Moon appears in September and the Hunter's Moon appears in October, but sometimes each appears a month later, and are sometimes confused.

The Blood Moon or Hunter's Moon has a relatively short time difference between moonrises on successive evenings, which lengthens the time when hunters can easily see the animals that come to glean the reaped fields -- and the foxes that come to prey on them.

While used in the "Old Farmer's Almanac" to refer to the Hunter's Moon, "Blood Moon" in the 21st century has come at NASA to describe a total lunar eclipse, due to the reddish tinge caused by Rayleigh scattering of sunlight through the Earth's atmosphere, the same phenomenon which also colors the sunset and gives the Harvest and Hunter's Moons their orange glow.

90. melanin

Melanin is the same pigment that determines a human's skin color and/or ability to tan. The agouti gene (A/a) controls the production and distribution of the pigment melanin in cats' hair. Black cats have the 'aa' genotype, which makes them appear solid black.

In these 'hypermelanistic' cats, the natural tabby pattern of domestic cats is hidden -- although a suggestion of it may appear as "ghost striping".

91. Samhain

They called it The Feast of the Dead, when those who had passed on came back and visited this world. It was the line between the Summer and the Winter months, when most things had been harvested.

92. Eighth century

Since October 31 was the day before All Hallow's Day, the night of October 31 had to be All Hallow's Eve, which in time became contracted to Halloween. The current date of All Saints' Day (All Hallow's Day) was founded by Pope Gregory, 731 to 741 AD.

93. Colcannon

Colcannon is a dish of mashed potatoes mixed with kale, and served with raw onions. Often boiled ham or Irish bacon will come with the dish. Kale comes into season in late fall and winter, so it's an ideal vegetable to have on Halloween.

94. Barmbrack Cake

Barmbrack cake is really a fruit bread, in which three "treasures" are baked. Everyone gets a piece of the cake. One lucky person gets a piece with a ring in it, denoting pending romance or continued happiness. Another gets a piece with a coin in it and can look forward to a prosperous year.

The last one, who gets a piece of rag, is not so lucky. His (or her!) financial picture ahead is "doubtful".

95. Turnips

According to the tale, Jack, an Irish blacksmith, made a pact with the Devil and therefore he was denied entry to Heaven. He was left to wander for eternity. When he asked for some light, he was given an ember which he put into a turnip he had hollowed out. Thus, the Irish kept one in their window to keep this damned soul, the Wandering Jack, out of their house.

When the Irish immigrated to America, pumpkins were far easier to find than were turnips, so they were used instead.

96. Spirits and devils

Since at Samhain the living and the dead were nearer to each other than at any other time in the year, the living were afraid that they might be carried away by the dead unless they disguised themselves to look like the dead looked. Or as they suspected the returning dead would look. That's why witches, goblins, ghosts and devils are the most popular costumes nowdays. Much the same as then.

97. Apple

In Ireland, that game is called "Snap Apple". Virtually the same game can be played by putting apples in a container of water and trying to get them out without using one's hands. That's called, in the US, "Bobbing for Apples".

98. A piece of hair

The idea is that after you do this, you go to sleep and you will dream of who your future spouse will be. The bonfire was one of the Celtic "fire" celebrations. (I assume only unmarried people do this...)

99. Throw dust at them

The Irish tradition says if you throw the dust from under your feet at the fairies and goblins that they will have to let loose all the souls that they had captured. So you'd be a real hero.

100. Spit on him

Now this tradition seems to have to do with farm animals, so I don't know whether or not you need to do it to your dog or cat. Perhaps you'd best roust your veterinarian out of bed so he can take a look. Holy water was often used on the animals, too, but that may be something of which you are presently out.

101. Summer's end

Samhain marked the beginning of harvest season when the farmers would reap their crops and slaughter livestock in preparation for winter. It was thought to be the Celtic New Year. The warding off of evil spirits was only a part of the Samhain festival.

102. UNICEF

The UNICEF program during Halloween began in the United States in 1950 in Philadelphia and expanded nationally in 1952. Teachers in schools distribute the collection boxes to their students, who in turn use them on Halloween night to solicit donations.

103. Turnip

Pumpkins are used in North America because they are more readily available and much larger than turnips. Jack-o'-lanterns are usually placed in windows or on the doorsteps of homes as a deterrent for evil spirits.

104. Jamie Lee Curtis

John Carpenter was the director of "Halloween". This was the debut movie role for

Jamie Lee Curtis. She became a major success as a result of her performance and was subsequently cast in a number of other horror films.

105.   Seelenwoche

Rituals include leaving out food and drink for spirits of ancestors returning for Halloween. Germans typically hide their knives in case spirits hurt themselves. Austrians in celebration of a successful harvest place a woven straw decoration on the outside of their doors. A black cat crossing one's path is considered particularly unlucky.

106.   Hasbro

The Ouija Board is a flat board marked with letters, numbers and other symbols used to communicate with the spirits. When the user places his hand on the indicator it apparently moves around the board to spell out messages. Parker Brothers first marketed this game in 1966, but the company was taken over by Hasbro in 1991.

107.   Macbeth

The extract depicts the three witches in the midst of concocting a stew containing blood, plants, frogs, bats, newts and various other animal parts. The witches would eventually play an important part in the tragic downfall of Macbeth.

108.   Thriller

Thriller was released in 1982. The album version of the song lasted just under six minutes, with the full video version released the following year, depicting dancing zombies, corpses and a frightening ambiance.

109.   Samhainophobia

The name of this fear has its origins in the old Celtic Festival of Samhain, generally regarded as the precursor to Halloween. This time of the year may stir up related phobias such as the fear of cats, witches, spiders, ghosts and cemeteries.

110.   Dan Rather

Dan Rather, born 1931, was best known as a journalist. Michael Landon (born 1936) was an actor. Sally Kirkland, born 1941, was an actress. Peter Jackson, the director, was born in 1961.

111.   All of these

Different countries have different ideas of how to destroy them.

112.   All Hallow's Eve

Halloween is the contracted corruption of All Hallow's Eve.

113.   Hocus Pocus

"Hocus Pocus" starred Bette Midler, Kathy Najami, and Sarah Jessica Parker as three witches come back from the dead after 300 years.

114.   Bat

Bats are traditionally the bad omen of this particular group...but, I don't know...a cockroach running around my house would sure scare me!

115.   Bobby Pickett

This song is definitely a favorite at Halloween parties!

116.   Full moon

I have no idea where this fable originated but it's a fun excuse to act crazy!

117.   Your financial outlook looks gloomy

The Barmbrack is a type of fruit and bread mix eaten by family members in Ireland during Halloween. Several objects are cooked into it, with each having a special significance. These are a rag, spotlessly clean of course, a coin and a ring. The coin signifies a prosperous year ahead, the ring of course continued happiness, or a new romance if single, and the rag a gloomy ahead for finances. Be careful when chomping into a piece of Barmbrack cake that you don't break your teeth!

118.   Colcannon

Colcannon, a word that translates to "cal ceannanan" in the Gaelic, means a white-headed cabbage. It is eaten with mashed potatoes and raw onion on Halloween in Ireland. After the potatoes are mashed, individual coins are wrapped up in greaseproof paper and put into each serving handed out to children. Imagine their delight upon spying same - and what a great way to ensure dinner is eaten.

119.   Colluding with Old Nick

Irish tradition has it that the art of carving pumpkins began in that lovely country.

Initially though, turnips were used instead of pumpkins. During the 1700s, one Jack the blacksmith was said to have colluded with the devil to obtain his objectives, and when this was revealed, he was forever after denied entry into heaven, and had to wander the earth eternally.

He asked his pitchforked cohort for some light to enable him to do this and was given a burning ember which he placed inside a hollowed out turnip.

When millions of Irish sailed to the United States to begin new lives in later years, this tradition went with them. Because of the scarcity of turnips there however, pumpkins were used instead. Today Jack O'Lanterns are placed in Irish windows on Halloween to keep Jack, that damned soul, away from the family home.

120.   Samhain

Halloween is the shortened version of the words "All Hallowtide" a time of the year associated with the pagan festival, Samhain, which the ancient Celts celebrated to mark the Feast of the Dead. During this time of the year which occurred at the end of summer and the beginning of the colder months, it was believed that the dead returned to revisit the world in which they had once dwelt.

By the 8th century, this festival continued to be celebrated in many countries worldwide, including Ireland, even though that country had well and truly converted to Christianity by then - and the Pope, the head of the church at that time, had had enough.

He created All Saints Day to counteract it, a day that is still celebrated by different denominations worldwide, to take place on the day after Halloween, to more or less head the pagans off at the pass.

121.   Dressing up in costumes

Because Halloween was the evening when the souls of the dead - and those still alive - were at their closest, and the belief that the devil also roamed about on that evening (you can't imagine how my Irish Catholic genes are quivering in terror here), the Irish began the tradition of dressing up in assorted costumes as a disguise so that that wicked person wouldn't recognise them and try to lure their souls away.

The spookier the costume, the better became the order of the day. Witches, ghouls and skeletons abounded.

These costumes, it was felt, would surely fool the wicked into thinking they belonged to them already.

122.   A cup of water

On the evening of Halloween in Ireland, an ivy leaf is put into a cup of water. This is then left overnight and checked the following morning for the results. If the ivy leaf is bobbing about, still green and healthy-looking, you are assured of twelve months of good health ahead. If, however, that leaf has developed brown spots overnight and is looking decidedly sick, then it is time to begin worrying.

123.   Suspended from a piece of string overhead

During the game of Snap Apple, a nice healthy apple is suspended from a piece of string over the heads of the children taking part in the game. They are then blindfolded, and, taking it in turns, have to try to take a bite out of the apple. The first child to get a decent bite out of the pome wins a prize.

This game can also be played by placing the apple in a large container of water, and, once again, blindfolded children have to try to get a bite from the elusive fruit.

124.   Throwing the dust under your feet at them

Irish fairies and goblins also try to steal souls away during this Irish Halloween tradition, and are very skilled at this crime. If, however, you meet any of these diabolical kidnappers on this evening, and you quickly gather up the dust from under your feet and throw it at them, then they are forced to release all the souls they are holding prisoner. Animals can also be protected from being whisked away as well by sprinkling them with Holy Water on this night, or, if looking a little poorly - obviously the work of those diabolical fairies and goblins - then you must quickly spit on them to protect them.

125.   A lock of their hair

Halloween bonfires are a delightful sight with the sparks flying high into air during a crisp cool evening, and in Ireland, these come with the added benefit of allowing young romantic hopefuls a vision of their future. By dropping a lock of their hair into the embers as the flames die down, it is believed that evening during sleep, they will dream of their future true love.

126.   Uprooting a cabbage

This Irish Halloween tradition has it that, on this spooky evening, if one goes out to a field, and uproots the first cabbage they find (while avoiding the irate farmer), this reveals his or her future married life. If the cabbage has a lot of earth remaining on its roots, the future spouse will own land and be well off. Otherwise, just between you and me, I'd bury it again and pull up another. Eating the cabbage will then reveal the nature of one's future love as well. Depending on its taste, that future life's partner will be either sour, bitter, or sweet.

127.   Samhain

To the ancient Celts, Samhain was a time of transition from summer to winter; it was a time to celebrate the harvest and prepare food for storage during the winter, which was considered to be the "darker half". They believed that during this time, the portals to the other world were opened, allowing the passage of dead souls, as well as fairies and elves, who became more active. While it may be true that Allhallowtide is descended from ancient Celtic traditions, My Lady assured us that it is a Christian tradition that was first approved by Pope Gregory IV. It evolved from the early "Feast of All Holy Martyrs", that was held in the spring, and moved to fall because, since it was harvest time, there would be more food available for pilgrims coming to Rome to worship. Of course, some say that the feast was moved to correspond with the pagan festival so that the beliefs could be easily merged. Authors Note: Historians are still debating the exact nature of the ancient Samhain event, as precise knowledge of Celtic religious rituals has not survived. It is known that the festival was held annually and animals were gathered in preparation for winter, however there is no evidence that it was also connected to honoring the dead. In reality, it was probably easier for the Christian church to win converts if an attempt was made to assimilate the old beliefs rather than abolish them.

128.   Turnip

During this time of the year, the ancient Celts believed the boundary between the world of the living and the world of the dead disappeared, and spirits of the dead could visit earth. We carve these lanterns, placing them on windowsills and carrying them with us, to help ward off any spirit that wishes to bring us harm, as well as to light our path. Some people believe they represent the spirits themselves, and help to guide them to their earthly homes. We also use mangelwurzels for lanterns.

Author's Note: Pumpkins became popular lanterns in North America because they are softer and easier to carve. Medieval Europeans, however, would not have known about this vegetable.

129.   Soul Cakes

Soul cakes are small, round cakes that are decorated with the mark of the cross. On All Hallow's Eve (remember many religious celebrations begin at sunset the night before) they are placed out as offerings for the dead, and for the next two days, the cakes, also called, "souls", are given to the poor and children, who go door to door begging for food. In exchange for the food, prayers are said for the dead souls in Purgatory, as well as for the family who provided the food.

Author's Note: Many believe this practice to be the origin of the modern trick or treating.

130.   Pouring egg whites into hot water

In all honesty, everyone looks forward to the fortune telling activities during Allhallowtide, and several methods are used. Young girls are told that if they look at their reflection at midnight, they will also see the image of the man they are to marry. Sometimes, however, a skull will appear which represents that the death of the girl will take place before marriage. Pouring egg whites or molten lead into water produces shapes that are then "interpreted" to tell one's future.

131.   Apples

The use of apples during Allhallowtide was, in all probability, incorporated into the Christian celebration from the Roman festival to honor Pomona. In fact, it is believed that the Romans introduced the apple tree sometime after their invasion of England!

The goddess of abundance, Pomona, protected gardens and orchards. She was not associated with the harvest, however, it was believed that she safeguarded the fruit and cultivation of the soil. One of our favorite activities during the season is to bob for apples that are either hanging from a string or placed in a tub of water; the first person to take a bite of the apple is the next allowed to marry. Special attention is also paid to the apple peeling - it is said that when an apple is skinned, the peeling will somehow show the initial of the man a girl is to marry!

132. **So the spirits will not recognize us**

We believe that the souls of Christians wander the earth during Allhallowtide and at this time, they have an opportunity to create grief or mischief for the living if they choose to do so. Wearing a costume ensures that if we are a target for such action, the spirits will not recognize who we are. We really don't spend much time making a costume; it is generally some sort of a mask that is used to cover our face.

133. **All Saints Day**

My Lady reminded us that we celebrate many days to honor saints, however, the purpose of All Saints Day is to insure that all of those martyrs who died in the name of Christ are venerated. Throughout the centuries so many died that it would be impossible to set aside a day to worship all of them (as had been the practice); in the 7th century Pope Boniface IV ordered an annual celebration to remember all the saints, and the Pantheon in Rome was rededicated in their honor.

134. **False**

The ancient Celts had no concept of the devil; they lit bonfires to honor and thank the sun god and recognize his growing powers in hopes that he would return in the spring. Only certain types of wood are burned, but other flammable items are burned to symbolically burn harmful influences. People lay near the fire and run through the smoke, using it as a cleansing ritual, The ashes from the fire are used by some to darken their faces and mask their identity.

Many people also extinguish the fire in their home, and relight it with a flame from the bonfire, or light a torch from the fire, carrying it around their homes and fields.

135.   Milk

Going back to the ancient Celts, November is the "blood month", where animals were butchered and the meat was preserved for the winter. We do not, however, pour blood on the graves. We use milk, or perhaps holy water. It is believed that this will help to appease the spirits who walk the earth so they will not commit any evil action against us.

Some people also set a place at their table for these spirits or leave food on their doorstep, as it is believed the spirits will visit their earthly home.

136.   Praying for dead Christians

Beginning in the 11th century as a day for monks to pray for the souls in Purgatory, today we all spend our time thinking about not only recently departed loved ones, but also those whose souls may still be in Purgatory. Ringing bells remind us to pray, but are also believed to comfort those in Purgatory who are awaiting further cleansing. Soul cakes are exchanged for prayers. Lit candles, called "soul lights" illuminate the otherwise gloomy surroundings in Purgatory.

137.   Buzz Lightyear

Buzz Lightyear is a character from the 'Toy Story' films. He also has a Saturday morning cartoon.

138.   Snow White

Too bad she didn't have seven smaller kids to follow her around!

139.   Cookie Monster and Oscar

My favorite 'Sesame Street' characters. I was Cookie Monster in the first grade! 'Sesame Street' has been on PBS for ... years.

140.   Alice (in Wonderland)

141.   Scooby Doo

Scooby Dooby Doo, where are you? Scooby Doo's name was inspired by a Frank Sinatra song.

142.   Darth Vader

Darth Vader from 'Star Wars' was voiced by James Earl Jones and said the infamous line 'No, I am your father' to Luke Skywalker.

143.   Ireland

Jack o' Lanterns originated in Ireland where it was common to place candles in hollowed-out turnips. This was done around the Samhain holiday in an attempt to keep away spirits and ghosts.

144.   Saint

Hallow means saint. The Catholic holiday of All Saints Day falls on November 1st and has become interwoven with other European holidays involving the coming of winter, the harvest season and the celebration of the dead to become the holiday that we know today.

145.   Tootsie Rolls

Tootsie Rolls can be found in almost any trick-or-treaters basket of candy and was the first penny candy to be individually wrapped. First produced in 1896, this inexpensive chocolate chewy candy was immensely popular and was even part of American soldiers' field rations during World War II.

146.   They wore masks and costumes

The ancient Celts would wear costumes with masks so that these evil spirits would not recognise them as humans. The variety of costumes and masks were as varied as those of today.

147.   River Phoenix

All of these men were born on October 31, except for River Phoenix. Instead, on Halloween of 1993 this 23 year old actor died of an alleged drug overdose.

148.   Spider

At one time, it was believed that it was good luck to see a spider on Halloween. It indicated that the spirit of a loved one was guarding you from evil spirits.

149.   Bobby "Boris" Pickett and the Crypt-Kickers

In 1962 Bobby "Boris" Pickett and the Crypt-Kickers recorded this holiday favorite.

Pickett imitates horror movie icon Boris Karloff throughout the song. The song is a narration by a mad scientist who creates a monster that, late one night, gets up and begins dancing. Numerous other musicians have recorded their own versions of the song including the Beach Boys, The Misfits, and the appropriately named musical group "Smashing Pumpkins".

150.   The peel was believed to land in the shape of the first letter of the future spouse

A young woman would throw an unbroken apple peel over her shoulder, believing that her futures spouse's first initial would appear. This was at a time when a good marriage was what most women aspired to. There was also another form of divination used for the same purpose. Northern European women were told that if they sat in a dark room Halloween night and looked in a mirror the face of her future husband would appear.

There were many variations of divination associated with Halloween by many different cultures.

151.   Samhainophobia

Samhainophobia is the fear of Halloween. It derives its name from the Irish festival of Samhain which celebrated the Celtic New Year as well as the Catholic All Saints' Day, and the Gaelic Festival of the Dead.

152.   True

You can make some really neat jack o' lanterns by using pumpkins that are naturally blue in color. They also come in a green variety and a white variety. This can make for a rainbow effect for your next Halloween!

153.   Samhain

154.   bat

155.   Salem, MA

156.   Egypt

157.   **Stake through the heart**

Garlic and crosses keep vampires away but only a stake through their heart will kill them. Sunlight is also said to kill them.

158.   **During a full moon**

159.   **they are slaves**

They wear chains because they are the slaves of their evil masters who have brought them to life using magic.

160.   **Europe**

HALLOWEEN TRIVIA :LEVEL DIFFICULT

161.   **What phobia do you suffer from if you have an intense fear of Halloween?**
a. Hallowphobia
b. Shamanphobia
c. Ghostphobia
d. Samhainophobia

162.   **What does the name Dracula mean?**
a. Blood drinker
b. Devil's son
c. Vampire Bat
d. Evil one

163.   **In Medieval times, what was commonly used as a cure for leprosy?**
a. a pumpkin
b. an apple
c. a broom bristle
d. a spider

164.   **Bobbing for apples began as a party game in the 20th Century?**
a. True
b. False

165.   **When did the UNICEF for Halloween program start?**
a. 1958
b. 1956
c. 1955
d. 1957

166.   **What U.S. city banned all Halloween celebrations from its schools in 1995**
a. Los Altos, California

b. Santa Fe, New Mexico
c. Philadelphia, Pennsylvania
d. Salt Lake City, Utah

167.   What does the word "witch" mean?
a. Evil one
b. Ugly one
c. Wicked one
d. Wise one

168.   Why does a witch commonly appear with a black cat?
a. For spell casting
b. For companionship
c. For protection
d. No reason

169.   What year did the Halloween novelty song "Monster Mash" reach number one on the Billboard charts?
a. never
b. 1967
c. 1962
d. 1965

170.   Halloween is always on October 31st.
a. True
b. False

171.   Tim Burton's "Nightmare Before Christmas" (1993), directed by Henry Selick tells a story about Halloween Town and Christmas Town. Who is the one who found the portal between the two towns?
a. Jack Skellington
b. Oogie Boogie the bogeyman
c. Sally the rag doll
d. Doctor Finklestein

172.   CSI: NY had an episode titled "Boo". This episode aired on October 31, 2007 and is the sixth episode in Season 4. What is the name of the town where the murders take place?
a. Castle Rock
b. Amityville
c. Salem
d. Witches Bend

173.   In the television special, "It's The Great Pumpkin, Charlie Brown", who does Snoopy battle?
a. Red Baron
b. Great Pumpkin
c. Vulture
d. Woodstock

174. **In 1982 the wonderful movie "E. T. The Extra-Terrestrial was released in theaters. Do you remember how E. T. was dressed for Halloween?**
a. Teddy Bear
b. Vampire
c. Ghost
d. Puppy

175. **Who was the author of the poem "The Witches Spell", a fun and popular Halloween poem?**
a. Walt Whitman
b. Edgar Allan Poe
c. Robert Frost
d. William Shakespeare

176. **In "Dark and Stormy Night", a 1994 episode from the television sitcom "Family Matters" Steve Urkel and the Winslow's play a story game, where they each play a part in the plot. Do you recall the name of this game?**
a. Pass the Ghost Story
b. Hide the Mummy
c. Blood or Guts
d. Murder at Midnight

177. **"Pooh's Heffalump Halloween Movie" (2005) is a delightful animated Walt Disney film. Why did Roo and Lumpy set out to find and catch the Gobloon.**
a. Tigger felt ill
b. Gobloon kidnapped Piglet
c. The Hundred Acre Woods became haunted
d. Pooh ate all of the candy

178. **Eddie Munster is a character on the television series "The Munsters". What interesting Halloween character does he represent?**
a. Quasimodo
b. Gargoyle
c. Warlock
d. Werewolf

179. **The "Monster Mash" by Bobby "Boris" Pickett was released in 1962. What was the name of the vocal group which was about to arrive, at this event, in the song?**
a. "The Crypt-Kicker Five"
b. "The Graveyard Ghouls"
c. "The Beastie Boys"
d. "The Transylvania Twist"

180. **"Garfield's Halloween Adventure" was first aired on October 30, 1985. Until the year 2000, this special was rerun every year. What does Garfield disguise himself as in costume?**
a. Pirate
b. Zorro
c. Clown
d. Dracula

181. **What was the reason for Michael Myers trying to kill Laurie Strode in the original "Halloween"?**
a. She made fun of him
b. Because she is his sister
c. We never find out why
d. She stole from him

182. **Who played The Shape in the original "Halloween"?**
a. Dick Warlock
b. Donald L. Shanks
c. Brad Loree
d. Nick Castle

183. **Who directed "Halloween: The Curse of Michael Myers"?**
a. Steve Miner
b. Dwight H. Little
c. Rick Rosenthal
d. Joe Chappelle

184. **Who directed "Halloween 3: Season of the Witch"?**
a. John Carpenter
b. Dwight H. Little
c. Rick Rosenthal
d. Tommy Lee Wallace

185. **In "Halloween 3: Season of the Witch" who played Daniel Challis?**
a. Tom Atkins
b. Conal Cochran
c. Michael Currie
d. Ralph Strait

186. **Who played Ellie Grimridge in "Halloween 3: Season of the Witch"?**
a. Jadeen Barbor
b. Nancy Kyes
c. Garn Stephens
d. Stacy Nelkin

187. **Who Wrote "Halloween 4: The Return of Michael Myers"?**
a. Larry Brand and Sean Hood

b.   Alan B. McElroy
c.   Robert Zappia and Matthew Greenberg
d.   Dwight H. Little

188.   Who played Deputy Nick Ross in "Halloween 5"?
a. Dave Ursin
b. Lance Guest
c. Frankie Como
d. Jeffrey Landman

189.   Who played Tina Williams in "Halloween 5"?
a. Jadeen Barbor
b. Tamara Glynn
c. Wendy Kaplan
d. Nancy Stephens

190.   Who was the director of photography for "Halloween 5"?
a. David Geddes
b. Peter Lyons Collister
c. Rob Draper
d. Billy Dickson

191.   The modern American concept of "Trick or Treating" originated from which organisation?
a. Candy Manufacturers
b. School boards
c. Retail Stores
d. Young Children

192.   Jack O'Lanterns were originally made from what?
a. celery
b. pumpkins
c. turnips
d. cherries

193.   Samhain is a word of _____ origin and is pronounced _____.
a. Italian: sa-mheen
b. French: sam-hayn
c. Celtic: sow-en
d. British: sam-hon

194.   Samhain was orginally celebrated when?
a.   Sheep Shearing Day
b. New Year's Eve
c. Summer Solstice
d. The Fool's Day

195.   How did Halloween get its name?
a.   It's always been called that
b. Evolved from All Hallow's Eve

c. Evolved from a popular greeting
d. None of these

Answers And Facts

161.   Samhainophobia

Halloween is the witches' New Year and is called Samhian.

162.   Devil's son

Bram Stoker's creation "Dracula" was based on the life of Prince Vlad Tepes (1431-1476). He was also called Vlad the Impaler since he had a bad habit of impaling his victims on stakes. The name "Dracula" is Romanian for Devil's son. Vlad Dracula's father was a knight of the Order of the Draco or dragon, so Dracula also translates as "the Son of Draco".

163.   a spider

A spider was rolled in butter and used as cure for diseases such as leprosy and the plague. Tasty!

164.   False

Bobbing for apples is a fertility rite, or a marriage divination and dates back to the Celtics. Unmarried people would try to bite into an apple floating in water or hanging from a string. The first person to bite into the apple would be the next one to marry.

165.   1955

The original idea started in 1950 in Philadelphia, when a Sunday school class had the idea of collecting money for needy children when trick-or-treating. They sent the money they made, about $17, to UNICEF (United Nations Children Fund), which was inspired by the idea and started a trick-or-treat program in 1955.

166.   Los Altos, California

The Los Altos, Ca., school system banned all Halloween celebrations because of the holiday's roots in pagan tradition.

167. **Wise one**

The word "witch" is derived from the word "wicca" which means wise one.

168. **For protection**

Black cats were originally believed to be witches' familiars who protected the witches' powers from negative forces.

169. **1962**

This great song written by Bobby "Boris" Pickett and Lenny Capizzi reached number one on the Billboard Charts for two weeks in 1962, and then returned to the charts in 1970 and 1973.

170. **True**

Have a Happy Halloween!

171. **Jack Skellington**

Jack Skellingon the "Pumpkin King" inadvertently finds the portal between Halloween Town and Christmas Town. Excited by his find and by the wonder that he saw in Christmas Town, he returns to Halloween Town and explains what he has found. The people of Halloween Town don't see it quite the same way, however. Playing along with the folks of Halloween Town, Jack finally announces that they would take over Christmas! Jack takes on the guise of Sandy Claws and rides a coffin pulled by skeletal reindeer! The real Santa is kidnapped and held prisoner by Oogie Booge. Sally tries to stop this terrible event and eventually Jack comes to his senses. Jack then helps Sally rescue Santa Claus. Romance blossoms between Jack and Sally with a wonderful happy ending to this animated film.

172. **Amityville**

The plot, of this part of the episode, centers on a slaughtered family in Amityville. The home, having been the scene where another family had died in a similar fashion, appears to be haunted. After DNA tests are done and past history of the previous murders is looked into, it is discovered that two people, Henry and Betty, had survived the past murders.

Henry and Betty did not want the new owners of the home to discover a suitcase full of bones which belonged to Henry's sister, whom he had accidentally shot years ago. Betty had hidden the body but when they learned that the new people were going to renovate the house, she wanted her child's bones back first.

While Henry was secretly in the house retrieving the bones, the family returned home early and that startled Henry! In his panic he shot all of them.

173.   Red Baron

"It's The Great Pumpkin, Charlie Brown" is a delightful animated television special, written by Charles M. Schulz. It first aired on October 27, 1966 and has been televised for very many years since then. Linus sits in the pumpkin patch all night waiting for the Great Pumpkin to appear. Snoopy makes his first appearance dressed up to battle the Red Baron, the famous World War I flying ace. Snoopy sits perched atop his doghouse doing battle while wearing his helmet, goggles and red scarf which was blowing in the wind.

174.   Ghost

E. T. was covered with a sheet and disguised as a ghost in the Halloween sequence from "E. T. The Extra-Terrestrial." The purpose of this was so that Elliott could sneak E.T. to the forest on his bicycle, in order for E. T. to be able to phone home. This wonderful film was written by Melissa Mathison. The director and co-producer was the renowned Steven Spielberg.

175.   William Shakespeare

In Act IV, Scene 1, from William Shakespeare's "Macbeth" (1606) comes the poem, "The Witches Spell".

1 WITCH) Thrice the brinded cat hath mew'd.

2 WITCH) Thrice and once, the hedge-pig whin'd.

3 WITCH) Harpier cries:-'tis time! 'tis time!

1 WITCH) Round about the caldron go;

In the poison'd entrails throw.-

Toad, that under cold stone,

Days and nights has thirty-one;

Swelter'd venom sleeping got,

Boil thou first i' the charmed pot!

ALL) Double, double toil and trouble;

Fire burn, and caldron bubble.

2 WITCH) Fillet of a fenny snake,

In the caldron boil and bake;

Eye of newt, and toe of frog,

Wool of bat, and tongue of dog,

Adder's fork, and blind-worm's sting,

Lizard's leg, and owlet's wing,-

For a charm of powerful trouble,

Like a hell-broth boil and bubble.

ALL) Double, double toil and trouble;

Fire burn, and cauldron bubble.

3 WITCH) Scale of dragon; tooth of wolf;

Witches' mummy; maw and gulf

Of the ravin'd salt-sea shark;

Root of hemlock digg'd i the dark;

Liver of blaspheming Jew;

Gall of goat, and slips of yew

Sliver'd in the moon's eclipse;

Nose of Turk, and Tartar's lips;

Finger of birth-strangled babe

Ditch-deliver'd by a drab,-

Make the gruel thick and slab:

Add thereto a tiger's chaudron,

For the ingrediants of our caldron.

ALL) Double, double toil and trouble;

Fire burn, and caldron bubble.

2 WITCH) Cool it with a baboon's blood,

Then the charm is firm and good.

176. Pass the Ghost Story

This takes place in season 6, episode 6 when a storm on Halloween night forces the cancellation of trick-or-treating, so to cheer up Richie, the characters take on the roles of a 19th-century vampire family. Carl and Harriette end up playing the parts of vampires wanting to bite the neck of Sir Steven, played by Urkel!

177. Pooh ate all of the candy

Roo's new friend, Lumpy, is really excited to go trick-or-treating for the first time, but Tigger tells Roo and Lumpy that there is an evil Gobloon in the forest and if he catches them he will turn them into Jaggedy Lanterns. Tigger adds that if they catch the Gobloon first, then they get to make a wish that will be granted to them.

Pooh ends up eating all of the candy so Roo and Lumpy set out to catch the Gobloon and get a wish for more candy granted to them. It doesn't quite go that way when the pair became separated.

178. Werewolf

Eddie Munster, played by actor Butch Patrick, in the television series "The Munsters" was the only child of Herman and Lily Munster. Eddie was a werewolf boy, and slept in either a coffin or a bureau drawer. His costume consisted of an exaggerated widow's peak, pointed ears, a "Little Lord Fauntleroy" suit and fangs. "The Munsters" television series first aired on September 24th, 1964. It ran a series of 70 episodes up until May 12th, 1966.

Extra note: Eddie was indeed a little werewolf, it is grandpa who was the vampire.

179. "The Crypt-Kicker Five"

Enjoy the lyrics and see for yourself, "The Crypt-Kicker Five" were the vocal group, indeed!

"Monster Mash" lyrics

I was working in the lab late one night

When my eyes beheld an eerie sight

For my monster from his slab began to rise

And suddenly to my surprise

He did the mash

He did the monster mash

The monster mash

It was a graveyard smash

He did the mash

It caught on in a flash

He did the mash

He did the monster mash

From my laboratory in the castle east

To the master bedroom where the vampires feast

The ghouls all came from their humble abodes

To get a jolt from my electrodes

They did the mash

They did the monster mash

The monster mash

It was a graveyard smash

They did the mash

It caught on in a flash

They did the mash

They did the monster mash

The zombies were having fun

The party had just begun

The guests included Wolf Man

Dracula and his son

The scene was rockin', all were digging the sounds

Igor on chains, backed by his baying hounds

The coffin-bangers were about to arrive

With their vocal group, "The Crypt-Kicker Five"

They played the mash

They played the monster mash

The monster mash

It was a graveyard smash

They played the mash

It caught on in a flash

They played the mash

They played the monster mash

Out from his coffin, Drac's voice did ring

Seems he was troubled by just one thing

He opened the lid and shook his fist

And said, "Whatever happened to my Transylvania twist?"

It's now the mash

It's now the monster mash

The monster mash

And it's a graveyard smash

It's now the mash

It's caught on in a flash

It's now the mash

It's now the monster mash

Now everything's cool, Drac's a part of the band

And my monster mash is the hit of the land

For you, the living, this mash was meant too

When you get to my door, tell them Boris sent you

Then you can mash

Then you can monster mash

The monster mash

And do my graveyard smash

Then you can mash

You'll catch on in a flash

Then you can mash

Then you can monster mash

180.   Pirate

Garfield dresses up as a pirate in his efforts to get twice as much candy and treats. He dresses Odie up as a pirate too and takes him along trick-or-treating. In his greed, Garfield sees more houses across the river and as they set out he orders Odie to "put out the oars". Odie understands that to mean he must throw the oars in the water. Adrift in the river they eventually reach land at a run-down old mansion where ghosts scare them and chase them.

They finally escape back into the river and wash to shore returning home where they end up sharing the candies they had collected earlier.

181.   We never find out why

This is sort of a trick question. Michael is trying to kill Laurie because she is his sister. But we don't find that out until "Halloween 2". In the original "Halloween" it is never once stated why Michael wants too kill Laurie Strode.

182.   Nick Castle

Nick Castle would later go on to co-write the script "Escape From New York" with John Carpenter.

183.   Joe Chappelle

Joe Chappelle has directed episodes of the short-lived TV series "Wolf Lake", and the movie "Skulls 2".

184.   Tommy Lee Wallace

Tommy Lee Wallace was the editor and production designer in the original "Halloween".

185. Tom Atkins

Tom Atkins also starred in the horror movies "Maniac Cop" and "The Fog". He also had a short stint playing an inmate on the 6th and final season of the HBO prison drama "Oz".

186. Stacy Nelkin

"Halloween 3: Season of the Witch" was produced by John Carpenter and Debra Hill.

187. Alan B. McElroy

Larry Brand and Sean Hood wrote "Halloween: Resurrection". Robert Zappia and Matthew Greenberg wrote "Halloween: H20", and Dwight H. Little directed "Halloween 4".

188. Frankie Como

Frankie Como spends some of his time working with a "Halloween" fan site.

189. Wendy Kaplan

Wendy Kaplan starred on the soap opera "The Guiding Light".

190. Rob Draper

Peter Lyons Collister was the director of photography on "Halloween 4: The Return of Michael Myers", Billy Dickson was director of photography on "Halloween: The Curse of Michael Myers", and David Geddes was director of photography on "Halloween" Resurrection".

191. School boards

Younger people were using Halloween as an excuse to commit pranks in the neighborhoods. As time went by, the pranks began to escalate into expensive vandalism, and in some cases violence. The school boards, urged to "do something" by the parents, got together with the town councils to come up with a safe activity for their children.

The town council, in turn, got the businesses and locals to all co-operate in giving the children candy, to keep them out of mischief.

192.   **turnips**

Jack O'Lanterns were put out to frighten away evil spirits. When pumpkins were discovered, they were found to be much easier to carve, thus the transition.

193.   **Celtic: sow-en**

Samhain marks the end of summer and beginning of winter in the Celtic tradition. The Celts only marked two seasons, summer and winter. Samhain means 'summer's end'. This day is used to communicate with and remember those who have passed on, as this is the time when the veil between the spirit world and the mundane world is at its thinnest. Samhain is celebrated October 31st, and is the holiday that Halloween derived from.

194.   **New Year's Eve**

Modern day pagans still celebrate Samhain. This is the time when they reflect over what has happened in the past year, and look forward to the growth they will have in the coming year. Those resolutions you make every December 31st to lose ten pounds next year come from these origins.

195.   **Evolved from All Hallow's Eve**

Christianity took the majority of its holidays from Pagan traditions, and renamed them. The Christians renamed this day "All Saint's Day." Since the Celts started their new day at sunset of the previous night, this became known as the evening of All Hallows (hallowed is a synonym for saint). From there it went to All Hallow's Eve, and then on to Halloween.

HALLOWEEN MOVIES

Halloween (1978)

196.   **Who did Laurie have a poster of on her wall?**
a.   Albert Einstein
b.   Mick Jagger
c.   Paul McCartney
d.   James Ensor

197.   **Who went up to the Myers' house on Halloween because of a dare?**
a.   Tommy Doyle

b. Annie Brackett
c. Lindsey Wallace
d. Lonnie Lamb

198. Who owned the house that Bob and Lynda used for their tryst?

a. The Strodes
b. The Wallaces
c. The Myers
d. The Bracketts

199. What did Laurie compare herself to when she was babysitting?

a. A mother
b. A day care worker
c. A girl scout
d. A slave

200. Why did Annie's boyfriend, Paul, get grounded?

a. Hey yelled at his parents.
b. He cheated on a test.
c. He got caught soaping windows.
d. He didn't finish his chores.

201. Where did Tommy hide to scare Lindsey?

a. Under the table
b. Behind the curtains
c. Lindsey was the one who scared Tommy
d. Under the bed

202. What costume did Lindsey Wallace wear?

a. A princess
b. She didn't wear a costume
c. An astronaut
d. A fairy

203. What was the model of the car that Michael stole to go to Haddonfield?

a. Station wagon
b. Jeep Wrangler
c. Ford F-150
d. He didn't steal a car

204. Who did Lynda think was driving the car that passed the girls on their way home from school?

a. Devon Graham
b. Paul
c. Michael Myers
d. Sheriff Brackett

205. Whose point of view did we see from at the start of the movie?

a. Laurie's
b. Lynda's
c. Annie's
d. Michael's

206. What two movies do Lindsey and Tommy watch throughout the course of the night?

a. "The Thing" and "Night of the Living Dead"
b. "The Exorcist" and "Forbidden Planet"
c. "The Thing" and "The Exorcist"
d. "The Thing" and "Forbidden Planet"

207. What is Lynda's last name?

a. Thompson
b. Van Derclork
c. Van Buren
d. Brackett

208. Annie's boyfriend's name is Bob.

a. True
b. False

209. Michael was adopted.

a. True
b. False

210. Annie was found dead in the closet.

a. True
b. False

211. In the beginning of the movie, Laurie's dad asks her to bring the key over to the Myers' place. Where does she put the key?

a. in the mail box
b. on the window sill
c. in the floor boards
d. under the mat

212. While Annie and Laurie are in the car, a song is playing. What is the name of this song?

a. The Halloween Theme
b. Don't Fear the Grave Keeper
c. The Monster Mash
d. Don't Fear the Reaper

213. What is the name of the doctor who works at Smith's Grove that supposedly let Michael leave the sanitarium?

a. Dr. Smith
b. Dr. Marion
c. Dr. Chambers
d. Dr. Wynn

214. What county is Michael supposed to see a judge in?
a. Haddon County
b. Harrisburg County
c. Russelsville County
d. Harden County

215. When Sheriff Brackett and Dr. Loomis go into the Myers house, they see something half dead on the floor. What is it?
a. a dog
b. a raccoon
c. a cat
d. a person

Halloween: The Night HE Came Home

216. From start to finish, what was the body count (not just people) in the original "Halloween"?
a. 7
b. 4
c. 6
d. 5

217. More fun with numbers: throughout parts 1 and 2, how many times is Michael presumed dead, only to get up again?
a. 4
b. 2
c. 5
d. 1

218. There were certain, subtle differences in Michael Myers himself between parts 1 and 2. Which of these is not one of those differences?
a. his walk
b. his main weapon
c. his mask
d. his motives

219. For different reasons, Michael is mistaken for someone else a couple of times in both movies. Who, among the following, is he not mistaken for?
a. Mr. Riddle
b. Bob
c. Bud
d. Sheriff Brackett

220. In part 2, when one of the nurses finds Dr. Mixter dead in his office, Michael slowly comes out of the shadows behind her and kills her with the help of what (think carefully)?

a.   kitchen knife
b.   fire
c.   water
d.   air

221.   Suppose they ran an autopsy on Michael at the end of part 2 (if he were dead, which of course he wasn't), which of these would the autopsy not reveal?
a.   one punctured eye
b.   several bullet wounds
c.   one amputated finger
d.   one puncture wound in the neck

222.   In part 1, in what house does Michael do most of his killing?
a.   the Strode house
b.   the Myers house
c.   the Wallace house
d.   the Doyle house

223.   At the start of part 2, how does Michael learn of Laurie's whereabouts?
a.   he hears it on the radio
b.   he is just drawn to her psychically
c.   he stows away in the ambulance
d.   he overhears some cops talking

224.   Which of these weapons was not used by Michael in either movie?
a.   hammer
b.   kitchen knife
c.   axe
d.   Scalpel

225.   Which character, introduced in part 1, was killed in part 2 ?
a.   Michael Myers
b.   Dr. Loomis
c.   Mr. Riddle
d.   Ben Tramer

The original Halloween Movie

226.   What was the name of Laurie's (Jamie Lee Curtis') best friend who was babysitting across the street in the original 'Halloween'?
a.   Lindsey Wallace
b.   Julie James
c.   Annie Brackett
d.   Judith Myers

227.   The character Michael Myers is named after a real person that John Carpenter actually knew.
a.   True

b.   False

228.   Who helped compose the 'Halloween' music, taking over for John Carpenter after he left the series?
a.   Jim Gillespie
b.   Steve Miner
c.   Debra Hill
d.   Alan Howarth

229.   What town did Marion live in at the beginning of 'Halloween H20'?
a.   Haddonfield, IL
b.   Langdon, IL
c.   Smith's Grove, IL
d.   Summer Glen, CA

230.   In 'H20', what is the name of the school that Keri Tate/Laurie Strode is the Headmistress of?
a.   Summer Glen Academy
b.   Hillcrest Academy
c.   Hollywood Hills Prep School
d.   Hillside Academy

231.   In 'Halloween 2', what kind of car does Karen drive?
a.   Chevy Camaro
b.   Monte Carlo
c.   Ford Mustang
d.   Dodge Dart

232.   At the end of part four, Jamie dresses in a clown costume and kills her step-mom.
a.   True
b.   False

233.   Name the two kids that Laurie and Annie are babysitting in the original 'Halloween'.
a.   Tommy & Leslie
b.   Timmy & Leslie
c.   Tommy & Lindsey
d.   Tony & Linda

234.   The name of the dog where Annie is babysitting in 'Halloween' is named Chester.
a.   True
b.   False

235.   What is Jamie's last name in 'Halloween 4'?
a.   Corruthers
b.   Lloyd
c.   Curtis
d.   Ellis

236.   **In 'Halloween 2' the young woman killed in the opening sequence is named:**
a. Ginny
b. Alice
c. Jill
d. Annie

237.   **Who is the character from 'Halloween' who returned in 'Halloween: The Curse of Michael Myers'?**
a. Lindsey
b. Annie
c. Tommy
d. Linda

238.   **Danny is Laurie son's name.**
a. True
b. False

239.   **What was the name of the farm the party in 'Halloween 5' is held at?**
a. Cornell Farm
b. Ellis Farm
c. Tower Farm
d. County Farm

240.   **The Original 'Halloween' was the highest grossing independent feature of all time until which of THESE movies topped it?**
a. 'Teenage Mutant Ninja Turtles'
b. 'Teen Wolf'
c. 'Goonies'
d. 'Gremlins'

Halloween: H20

241.   **Which wound did Sarah not acquire before being hung on the light in the storage room?**
a. Multiple stabbings
b. Her leg being cut
c. A broken collarbone
d. A broken leg

242.   **Which actor did not act in this movie?**
a. Janet Leigh
b. Jodi Lyn O'Keefe
c. Donald Pleasence
d. Nancy Stephens

243.   What was the reference to "Halloween 5: The Revenge of Michael Myers" in this movie?
a.   There was a group picture of the whole cast on Loomis's bed.
b.   There was no reference.
c.   There was a picture of bloody scissors in Loomis's room.
d.   There was a picture of young Jamie Lloyd on Laurie Strode's desk.

244.   Which was not a style of killing used in this movie?
a.   knife in back
b.   gunshot wound
c.   hockey skate through face
d.   slashed throat

245.   Which did Michael not have to endure in this movie?
a.   A knife in the back
b.   A fire extinguisher to the head
c.   A beating with a fire poker
d.   A rock to the head

246.   What city did Marion Wittington live in?
a.   Haddonfield, Illinois
b.   Chicago, Illinois
c.   It is never revealed.
d.   Langdon, Illinois

247.   What had Jimmy been suspended for "five times this year"?
a.   "Gettin' a little crazy with the stick!"
b.   "Havin' a little too much fun during lunchtime!"
c.   "Not paying attention in class!"
d.   "Egging every classroom possible!"

248.   What did Tony suggest that he and Jimmy do to the house across the street?
a.   "TP it."
b.   "Egg it."
c.   "Throw rocks at it."
d.   Nothing

249.   What was the name of the mother at the rest stop in this movie?
a.   Marcia
b.   Claudia
c.   Cynthia
d.   Jessica

250.   What did the little girl at the rest stop think she saw, and what was her name?
a.   cockroaches/Janey
b.   spiders/Casey
c.   spiders/Janey

d. crickets/Casey

251.   Who is the Music Supervisor?
a. Ed Gerrard
b. John Ottman
c. Debra Hill
d. Matt Moreman

252.   Who played as Jimmy?
a. Joshua Jackson
b. Fred Durst
c. Justin Timberlake
d. Joseph Gordon-Levitt

253.   Who is the Costume Designer?
a. Deborah Everton
b. Jamie Lee Curtis
c. John Carpenter
d. Debra Hill

254.   What other movie did LL Cool J play in?
a. Scream
b. B.A.P.S.
c. The Great Outdoors
d. The Mask

255.   Near the beginning, what is the little girl screaming about?
a. cockroaches
b. grasshoppers
c. ants
d. spiders

256.   Approximately how long is the video cassette?
a. 86 minutes
b. 110 minutes
c. 86 hours
d. 90 minutes

257.   What is the number and the name on the jersey Tony, Jimmy's friend, was wearing?
a. 17, ALLEGRE
b. 17, ALBERT
c. 17, ALEGRA
d. 17, ANDERSON

258.   What does Charlie say to Michael in the kitchen?
a. hello
b. what's up
c. hi

d.   bye

259.   Which Creed song is played in this movie?
a.   What's This Life For
b.   What If
c.   Higher
d.   Torn

260.   How many buses did the school take to Yosemite?
a.   three
b.   two
c.   one
d.   six

261.   Who does Annie talk to Laurie about?
a.   Sam
b.   Paul
c.   Ben
d.   Bob

262.   According to Chester Chesterfield, Deborah Myers committed suicide. What does he say she couldn't take being labeled as?
a.   Satan's Mom
b.   Psycho Mom
c.   Mother of Frankenstein
d.   Mommy Dearest

263.   How does Annie die?
a.   Annie does not die.
b.   Michael stabs Annie in the throat with a kitchen knife.
c.   Michael breaks Annie's neck.
d.   Michael kills Annie with a fireplace poker to the stomach.

264.   What does Lindsay dress up as for Halloween?
a.   Princess
b.   Ballerina
c.   Queen of Sheba
d.   Witch

265.   What does Laurie fix Tommy to eat?
a.   fat free yogurt
b.   ham sandwich no cheese
c.   jelly sandwich
d.   tuna without mayonnaise

266.   Who plays the clerk at the gun store?
a.   Mickey Dolenz
b.   Brad Douriff
c.   Skyler Gisondo
d.   Adam Weisman

267.   What does Doctor Koplenson tell Dr. Loomis?

a.   Koplenson says, "Michael has raped a girl in the institution".

b.   Koplenson says, "Michael has been released on parole".

c.   Koplenson says, "Michael has driven away in the middle of the night".

d.   Koplenson says, "He is out.".

268.   Where do Loomis and Sheriff Brackett meet for the first time?

a.   Joe's of Haddonfield

b.   Haddonfield Burger

c.   Haddonfield Joe's Premium Subs

d.   Subway

269.   Why is Paul grounded?

a.   Paul crashed his dad's car.

b.   Paul crashed his dad's motorcycle.

c.   Paul stole money from his mom's wallet.

d.   Paul stole alcohol from his parent's house.

270.   What station does Taylor Madison work for?

a.   WNKW

b.   WBAL

c.   WJZ

d.   MSNBC

271.   What does Joe call Michael?

a.   Sally

b.   Goober

c.   Michele

d.   Daisy

272.   What does Cynthia make for breakfast?

a.   oatmeal

b.   waffles

c.   pancakes

d.   eggs

273.   What type of business does Mason own?

a.   real estate

b.   auto dealership

c.   home improvement

d.   convenient store

274.   What does Annie call Laurie?

a.   Joan of Arc

b.   Mother Teresa

c.   Saint Laurie

d.   She calls her an angel.

275.   How does Cynthia die?

a.   Michael kills her by crushing her skull.

b.   Michael stabs her with a fireplace poker.

c.   Michael snaps her neck.

d.   Michael cuts her throat with a knife.

276.   What does Linda say her dad calls her?

a.   Angel

b.   Pookie

c.   Sweetie

d.   Pumpkin

277.   How does Bob die?

a.   He is decapitated.

b.   He is stabbed.

c.   He is suffocated by a plastic bag.

d.   He is strangled with a telephone cord.

278.   Who plays Chester Chesterfield?

a.   Rob Zombie

b.   Clint Howard

c.   Brad Dourif

d.   Sid Haig

279.   What scream queen plays Cynthia Strode?

a.   Dee Wallace Stone

b.   Jennifer Love Hewitt

c.   Jamie Lee Curtis

d.   Neve Campbell

280.   What does Michael do to Paul?

a.   Michael slashes Paul open and hangs him from the ceiling.

b.   Michael cuts Paul's eyes out with a knife.

c.   Michael pins him to a the wall with a knife.

d.   Michael puts a pumpkin on his head.

Halloween 2

281.   What movie are the Elrod's watching in the opening scene?

a.   Night of the Living Dead

b.   Day of the Dead

c.   Dawn of the Dead

d.   Return on the Living Dead

282.   What is Jimmy's brother's name?

a.   Bobby

b.   Iggy

c.   Ziggy

d.   Marty

283. **What is the name of the TV station that is doing most of the broadcasting in Haddonfield?**

a. WKRA

b. RKWA

c. KRWA

d. WWAR

284. **What is the name of the teenager who gets hit and blown up by the police car?**

a. Ben Tramer

b. Dan Tramer

c. Sam Tramer

d. Joe Tramer

285. **What was the name of the reporter from the TV station that is doing most of the broadcasting in Haddonfield?**

a. Steven Canady

b. Dan Anderson

c. Martin Malloy

d. Robert Mundy

286. **What is the make of the ambulance shown in the beginning of this film?**

a. Ford

b. GMC

c. Chevy

d. Dodge

287. **What show is Mr. Garrett watching when Karen shows up for work?**

a. The Bad Seed

b. Dementia

c. Psycho

d. The Thing

288. **What is the name of the small gift shop that Dr. Loomis passes while riding in the Marshall's car with Marion?**

a. The Keeper

b. The Keeping

c. Keepers

d. The Keepsake

289. **What color is Karen's convertible?**

a. Silver

b. Black

c. Red

d. White

290.   **Towards the end of the movie, Laurie shoots Michael. What part of Michael's body does she shoot?**

a.   eyes
b.   arm
c.   chest
d.   Stomach

291.   **Annie told her dad to bring pizza home for dinner for the family. What kind of crust did she tell him to get?**

a.   thin crust
b.   stuffed crust
c.   whole wheat
d.   unbleached flour crust

292.   **What kind of mask did Big Lou wear?**

a.   Dracula
b.   Creature from the Black Lagoon
c.   Wolf man
d.   Frankenstein

293.   **What character from "The Rocky Horror Picture Show" did Laurie dress as?**

a.   Columbia
b.   Dr. Frank-N-Furter
c.   Riff Raff
d.   Magenta

294.   **What was Laurie's birth name?**

a.   Samantha
b.   Saundra
c.   Andrea
d.   Angel

295.   **What was the name of the store Laurie worked at?**

a.   Uncle Meat's Music and More
b.   Uncle Meat's Java Hole
c.   Uncle Meat's Indie Books and Music
d.   Uncle Meat's Hemp House

296.   **We saw Deborah Myers throughout the entire film as a ghost. What kind of animal was with Deborah in the movie?**

a.   white dove
b.   white dog
c.   white rabbit
d.   white horse

297.   **Why did the men in the truck beat Michael?**

a.   They recognized Michael and wanted to turn him in for the reward money.

b. They thought Michael was the man who raped one of their daughters.
c. They thought he was homeless and stealing from them.
d. They thought Michael was the one who killed their cattle.

298. Which parent of a victim from the previous film tried to shoot Dr. Loomis in this film?
a. Lynda's mom
b. Wesley's mom
c. Wesley's dad
d. Lynda's dad

299. What was Annie doing before Michael killed her?
a. Annie was washing and putting away dishes.
b. Annie was taking out the trash.
c. Annie was getting ready to brush her teeth.
d. Annie was taking a shower.

300. Who was holding Laurie down when the helicopter flew over the shack she was in?
a. Young Michael
b. Nobody
c. Adult Michael
d. Deborah

Answers And Facts

196. James Ensor

Laurie had a poster of James Ensor on her wall. James Ensor was a painter who often did work about men wearing grotesque masks. It was of course ironic because Michael was a man in a grotesque mask. Laurie came home from school, still a bit jumpy from her eerie walk home. When she walked around her room you could clearly see the poster of James on the wall.

197. Lonnie Lamb

Lonnie Lamb, the boy who bullied Tommy, went up to the Myer's house as his friends cheered him on. Loomis was waiting for Michael behind the bushes and taught Lonnie a lesson. As Lonnie got on the porch Loomis said, "Hey Lonnie, get your ass away from there," in a creepy voice. Lonnie and his friends ran fast.

198. The Wallaces

Bob and Lynda walked into the Wallace house thinking Annie and Lindsey would be there. They were surprised to find the house empty (unbeknownst to them that Annie was dead, and Lindsey was with Laurie). They kissed on the Wallaces' couch and quickly made their way up to the bedroom. They made themselves at home not knowing that it would become the place of their deaths.

199.   A girl scout

Laurie, who was working on a jack-o-lantern for Tommy, got off the phone with Annie, who had asked her to watch Lindsey so she could go see her boyfriend. Laurie agreed and commented to herself that "the old girl scout comes through again".

200.   He got caught soaping windows.

On their way home from school the girls discussed their plans for that night. Annie said Paul "got caught soaping windows" and was grounded. We never actually saw Paul in the movie but we heard his voice when he was on the phone with Annie. The voice that can be heard was that of the director, John Carpenter.

201.   Behind the curtains

Tommy wanted to scare Lindsey so he quietly got off the couch, went behind the curtains and said "Lindsey" in a scary voice. But the real joke was on Tommy who looked out the window behind him to see Michael, scaring him and causing him to scream. Lindsey wasn't mad at Tommy and even believed him when he told Lindsey and Laurie that he had seen the boogie man.

202.   She didn't wear a costume

Lindsey Wallace was never shown wearing a costume, but rather a plaid dress and a red t-shirt. Her friend, Tommy Doyle, dressed as an astronaut.

203.   Station wagon

Michael had escaped from Smith's Grove in a state plated station wagon originally driven by his new nurse, Marion. Michael jumped on the car, broke the window and forced Marion out. Dr. Loomis was understandably surprised to see a man who had been locked up since the age of six drive away. The station wagon even had a state sticker on the side.

204.   **Devon Graham**

When walking home from school the girls saw a station wagon going down the street. When the girls wondered who was driving, Lynda said, "Is that Devon Graham?" Laurie said, "I don't think so". To that, ditzy Lynda said, "I think he's cute". The person who was actually driving was Michael.

205.   **Michael's**

In the first scene of the movie, we saw Michael's point of view as a six year old boy. He was dressed as a clown and he was spying on his sister. When her boyfriend left, Michael grabbed a butcher knife, walked upstairs and killed his sister. When he walked outside the camera panned to show his face.

206.   **"The Thing" and "Forbidden Planet"**

"Night of the Living Dead" wasn't shown until the second "Halloween", and "The Exorcist" was never shown in the movie.

207.   **Van Derclork**

Brackett was Annie's last name, and the other two were made up.

208.   **False**

Lynda's boyfriend was Bob. Annie's boyfriend was Paul.

209.   **False**

Michael was not adopted. Laurie was adopted by the Strodes. Laurie Strode was really a Myers.

210.   **False**

Annie was on the bed, and Lynda was the one in the closet.

211.   **under the mat**

Laurie goes up to the house even though Tommy warns her that it's haunted.

212.   **Don't Fear the Reaper**

This song was also used in the movie "Scream". The original version of the song is being played in "Halloween", though.

213.   Dr. Wynn

Dr. Loomis talks with Dr. Wynn about how Michael got out, and Dr. Wynn obviously didn't know how dangerous Michael was.

214.   Harden County

When Dr. Loomis and Marion Chambers are talking in the car, she asks him why Michael has to go all the way to Harden County to see the judge, and Dr. Loomis says, "Because it's the law."

215.   a dog

They soon realize that it's a dog, and Dr. Loomis says, "He got hungry."

216.   7

Five people and two dogs lose their lives. At the beginning, Michael kills his sister (1), then when Michael escapes from the asylum, Dr. Loomis finds a Phelps Garage tow truck with a dead mechanic (2), in the Myers house, Dr. Loomis and the sheriff find a butchered dog (3), Michael kills Lester the dog outside the Wallace house (4), later Michael kills Annie in her car (5), then he knifes Bob in the kitchen of said house (6), and finally, he strangles Lynda with a phone cord (7).

217.   5

The first time is in the original, when Laurie sticks a knitting needle in his neck, then again when she stabbs him with his own knife in the closet, then at the end, Dr. Loomis shoots him down and he walks away. The next time is towards the end of part 2, after they blast him again, he proceeds to scalpel the first guy who checks his pulse.

The last time is when Dr. Loomis blows him (and himself) up at the end, Michael starts walking while on fire. He only walks for a little bit, I know, but nevertheless, nobody expects him to get up and try to walk off the explosion.

218.   his motives

First of all, the mask in part 2 doesn't look quite like part 1 (which is all supposed to occur the same night). This may only be due to wear and tear between the making of the two movies, but the mask does look different nonetheless. Secondly, whereas in part 1, Michael's main hand-held weapon was the butcher knife, since he was in a hospital he spent most of part 2 walking around with a scalpel. Finally, in part 1, his walk was a lot more predatory, he seems lighter on his feet.

In part 2 (due to a new director and actor playing Michael) he looks more like he's just ambling along. Compare Michael walking down the stairs in part 1 with him doing the same in part 2. If Michael chased Laurie through the hospital basement at the pace he walked in part 1, he would have killed her easily.

His motive was always the same, we just didn't know what it was until the sequel.

219.   **Sheriff Brackett**

In part one, when Laurie is telling Annie about seeing Michael in her backyard, Annie replies that it must be the neighbor, Mr. Riddle. Later, Michael kills Lynda while passing himself off as Bob, by wearing a sheet on his head like a ghost. Finally in part 2, right before Michael drowns the girl in the hot tub, he walks up from behind and she believes he's her boyfriend Bud.

220.   **air**

Technically, Michael plunged an empty syringe into her temple, but what actually killed her was the air inside of it. Out of the choices above, it was the logical answer. I had to make it interesting.

221.   **one amputated finger**

Laurie stabbed him in the neck and later, in the stomach with a knife. She also stabbed him the eye with a knitting needle. He was shot a few times, mostly by Dr. Loomis. The coroner would actually find BOTH of his eyes gone, from when Laurie put a bullet in each one at the end of part 2.

222.   **the Wallace house**

Annie was babysitting Lindsey Wallace. She sent Lindsey to stay with Laurie and Tommy Doyle, and was soon killed in her car behind the Wallace house. Michael then carried her body into the house and waited for fresh victims. Sure enough, in came Bob and Lynda (soon dead), and later on, Laurie came around too, though she made it out alive.

223.   **he hears it on the radio**

Early on, we see a shot of a kid walking down the street with his boombox on his shoulder, (oddly) listening to the radio news. The report is on a series of murders in Haddonfield, and he bumps into Michael just as they mention that one survivor was taken to Haddonfield Memorial Hospital.

224.   **axe**

The kitchen knife is, of course, his modus operandi. The hammer found its way into the hospital security guard Mr. Garrett's skull early in part 2. The scalpel pretty much replaced the kitchen knife as Michael's carry-around tool in part 2. Michael never used an axe, at least he didn't until the disgraceful "Halloween 6".

225.   **Ben Tramer**

OK, so it's a kind of a cheap question. Ben was not actually seen in part 1, only mentioned (Laurie told Annie she had a thing for him). In part 2, when the teenager in the Michael Myers mask gets run over by a car, we later find out that his name is... Ben Tramer! Michael Myers and Dr. Loomis were presumed dead, but actually survived to be in subsequent sequels. If you got this one right, you qualify as a hardcore "Halloween" buff.

226.   **Annie Brackett**

Annie was her best friend in the original. In real life Jamie Lee Curtis' daughter is named Annie. Coincidence?

227.   **True**

Michael Myers was an aquantance of John Carpenter and Debra Hill. He passed away in the late 90's.

228.   **Alan Howarth**

Alan Howarth took over for John. Jim Gillespie is the director of 'I Know What You Did Last Summer'. Debra Hill was John's partner for writing and producing the first two 'Halloween' movies. And Steve Miner directed 'H20'.

229. **Langdon, IL**

Smith's Grove was where the institution was in earlier films. Summer Glen is where Laurie/Keri lived in 'H20'. And Haddonfield? Do you have to ask?

230. **Hillcrest Academy**

The house that they used for the school in 'H20' is also doubled as John Milton's house in 'Scream 3'. There is a legend about the house involving some grizzly murders.

231. **Ford Mustang**

Karen drove a Ford Mustang. The Monte Carlo was Annie's in part one. The Dodge Dart was Leslie's in part 4. The Camaro was Michael's (Tina's boyfriend) in part 5.

232. **False**

We learn in part five that Jamie stabbed her, but didn't kill her. Rachael says they are at the cottage and they send their love to Jamie.

233. **Tommy & Lindsey**

Tommy Doyle and Lindsey Wallace.

234. **False**

The dog's name is actually Lester.

235. **Lloyd**

In 'Halloween 5' her name is Corruthers. Meaning she must have been adopted between 4 and 5.

236. **Alice**

237. **Tommy**

In 'Halloween', he was played by Brian Andrews. In 'The Curse...', he is played by Paul Rudd.

238. **False**

John was Laurie's son's name. Danny was Kara's son's name in 'The Curse...'

239. **Tower Farm**

240. **'Teenage Mutant Ninja Turtles'**

241.   **A broken collarbone**

As she was closing the dumbwaiter door, Michael slashed her leg with his knife. Then, as she was getting out of the dumbwaiter, Michael cut the pulley rope, causing the dumbwaiter to fall, crushing her leg. She was then stabbed four times by Michael.

242.   **Donald Pleasence**

Jodi Lyn O'Keefe played Sarah (girlfriend of Charlie and best friend of Molly). Nancy Stephens's character, Marion Wittington, was short-lived at the beginning of the movie. Janet Leigh played Norma, Laurie Strode's/Keri Tate's character's secretary. Donald Pleasence was seen in a couple of pictures, but that was it.

243.   **There was a picture of bloody scissors in Loomis's room.**

When we were shown Loomis's bedroom, there was a picture of a bloody pair of scissors. The note next to it said something like "Punctured aorta". The aorta is in your heart, and Michael Myers stabbed Rachel Corruthers in "Halloween 5" with a pair of scissors...in her heart.

244.   **gunshot wound**

The first two people to die in the movie, Jimmy and Tony, were killed with the "hockey skate through face" and "knife in back" tactics respectively. Will Brennan also was killed in a "knife in back" style. Charlie had his throat slashed. Ronnie (LL COOL J's character) was shot at, and a bullet did graze his ear, but he wasn't killed.

245.   **A knife in the back**

We saw all of these on the screen. The beating, he got from Marion Wittington in the first scene. The fire extinguisher, he got from Laurie Strode in part of the climax. The rock, he got from Molly, when they were running outside. He was the one who normally did the stabbing with the knife in the back, but it never happened to him in this movie.

246.   **Langdon, Illinois**

Haddonfield, if it was chosen as an answer, was probably done so because the first six movies had something to do with that town. Chicago is just another very famous city in Illinois. At the very beginning of the movie, the first bit of text shown on the screen was "Langdon, Illinois".

This was shown following a mom carving a pumpkin and before the audience seeing Marion Wittington for the first time since "Halloween 2".

247.   "Gettin' a little crazy with the stick!"

While he was investigating Marion's house, he said this as a threat to whoever was in there. This was said as he was walking down the main hallway of her house. He later heard a creak in the house and got scared.

248.   "Egg it."

Although it was said very quietly, turning up the volume or adding captions to the movie would have allowed the viewer to see or hear this very clearly. This was said when Jimmy and Tony were leaving Marion's house (after Jimmy stole some booze).

249.   Claudia

Never was her name verbally said, but she was listed in the credits. Only the truly die-hard fans...or the obsessors like me...would catch this minor detail.

250.   spiders/Casey

As Claudia and Casey were doing their business, Claudia looked down at the purse that she left on the floor of the bathroom stall. She then saw Michael's hand reach down and grab it. Naturally, she started freakin' out! As Casey was in the next stall singing "Mary Had a Little Lamb", Claudia heard a scream.

She rushed to the next stall only to find that Casey was a little wigged by some spiders that she saw.

251.   Ed Gerrard

Ed Gerrard is the music supervisor for the movie Halloween H20. As a music supervisor, Gerrard was responsible for selecting and licensing the music used in the film. Interestingly, Gerrard has worked on several other horror movies, including Scream and I Know What You Did Last Summer.

In addition to his work in film, Gerrard has also worked as a music supervisor for television shows such as Dawson's Creek and The O.C. His expertise in selecting music that enhances the mood and tone of a scene has made him a sought-after professional in the entertainment industry.

252. Joseph Gordon-Levitt

Joseph Gordon-Levitt played as Jimmy in Halloween H20. Interestingly, Gordon-Levitt began his acting career as a child actor and has since become a well-known actor in Hollywood. He has received numerous accolades for his performances, including a Golden Globe nomination for his role in (500) Days of Summer.

In addition to his acting career, Gordon-Levitt is also a writer, director, and producer. He founded the online production company, HitRecord, which allows artists to collaborate on various projects.

253. Deborah Everton

Deborah Everton is a highly skilled costume designer who has worked on numerous films and TV shows. She is known for her attention to detail and ability to create costumes that perfectly capture the essence of a character. In the case of Halloween H20, Everton was tasked with designing costumes that would help bring the iconic horror movie to life.

Her work on the film helped to create a sense of realism and authenticity that helped to make the movie a classic of the genre.

254. B.A.P.S.

LL Cool J also appeared in the 1999 comedy film B.A.P.S., which stands for Black American Princesses. The movie follows two waitresses from Georgia who travel to Los Angeles to audition for a music video, but end up being mistaken for heirs to a fortune. LL Cool J plays the role of a wealthy man who becomes romantically involved with one of the waitresses.

Despite receiving negative reviews from critics, B.A.P.S. has gained a cult following over the years.

255. spiders

Arachnophobia is a common fear among people, and it's not surprising that spiders are often portrayed as scary creatures in movies. In Halloween H20, a little girl screams about spiders, adding to the suspense and fear of the scene. Interestingly, spiders are not only feared by humans, but they also play an important role in the ecosystem by controlling insect populations.

Some species of spiders are even kept as pets by enthusiasts.

256.   86 minutes

The video cassette of Halloween H20 has a runtime of 86 minutes. Interestingly, this movie marked the return of Jamie Lee Curtis to the Halloween franchise after a 17-year absence. It also features a cameo by her mother, Janet Leigh, who famously starred in the classic horror film Psycho. Halloween H20 was a box office success, grossing over $55 million domestically, and is considered by many fans to be one of the best sequels in the Halloween series.

257.   17, ALLEGRE

Tony, Jimmy's friend, was wearing the number 17 jersey with the name ALLEGRE on the back in the movie Halloween H20. Interestingly, the name ALLEGRE is a reference to the film's producer, Malek Akkad's wife, Nancy Allegre. The number 17 is also significant as it is the same number worn by Laurie Strode, the main character played by Jamie Lee Curtis, in the original Halloween film.

This small detail serves as a nod to the franchise's history and adds to the overall nostalgia of the movie.

258.   hi

259.   What's This Life For

"What's This Life For" by Creed is played in the movie Halloween H20. The song was released in 1998 as the second single from their debut album, My Own Prison. Interestingly, the song was written by lead vocalist Scott Stapp when he was only 18 years old and deals with the theme of searching for the meaning of life.

It's fitting that the song was used in a horror movie, as the lyrics also touch on the fear of death and the unknown. The song's inclusion in Halloween H20 adds to the film's intense and emotional climax.

260.   three

261.   Ben

Annie drops Lindsay off at Tommy's house. Laurie is going to watch Lindsay for Annie while Annie goes out on a date with her boyfriend, Paul. Annie tells Laurie she talked to Paul about Ben for Laurie. Annie says that Ben said Laurie is hot. Annie tells Laurie she needs a boyfriend and Laurie says she doesn't. The girls then start to joke around in front of the kids. Paul pulls up and Annie goes outside to meet him.

Ben Tramer is also a name used in the original "Halloween". His character is killed off in the second part of the series. Paul is Annie's boyfriend. Bob is Lynda's boyfriend. Sam is Doctor Samuel Loomis, Michael's psychiatrist.

262.   Satan's Mom

Chester is taking Samuel to the grave site of Judith Myers. He starts to tell the story of the Myers' tragedy to Loomis. Chester tells Sam that Deborah could not handle being labeled Satan's mom and killed herself. Chester also makes a comment in regards to the doctor on the case. Chester says the doctor wrote a book, but Chester does not know that Loomis is Michael's doctor. Chester tells Loomis that the book is blood money. Sam says, "I read that book and it was a masterpiece". Chester and Loomis approach Judith's grave and find her tombstone missing.

263.   Annie does not die.

Laurie is walking Lindsay back over to her house. Laurie calls in the house to Annie and tells her she better be decent. Laurie asks Lindsay to turn on the light. Lindsay turns on the light and screams. Paul is hanging dead from the ceiling with a pumpkin on his head. Laurie sees Annie lying bloody on the floor. Laurie tells Lindsay to run home and call the police. Laurie goes into the kitchen and dials the police as well. Michael is behind the door and closes it as Lindsay leaves. Annie starts to call out to Laurie to warn her that Michael is coming.

264.   Queen of Sheba

Annie calls over to Tommy's house to speak to Laurie. Annie tells Laurie she will be bringing the Queen of Sheba over soon. Annie walks into the living room where

Lindsay is watching television, and tells her to come on they are going to see Tommy. Annie and Lindsay walk over to Tommy's house. Annie is carrying a pumpkin for Lindsay, and Lindsay is carrying a bowl of popcorn Annie made for her.

When Laurie tells Lindsay it is time to leave, Tommy tells her to get out. Lindsay tells Tommy who does he think he is talking to. Lindsay says she is the Queen of Sheba and he needs to bow down and worship her.

265.   jelly sandwich

Laurie brings Tommy's sandwich to him at the dinner table. She tells him it is a jelly sandwich hold the peanut butter. He tells her that if she would have listened to him, she would not have had to make it twice. Laurie serves Tommy's sandwich with a side of chips. Tommy then starts to ask Laurie about the bogeyman. Laurie tells Tommy there is no such thing.

266.   Mickey Dolenz

Dr. Loomis is in the gun store trying to buy a gun. He sees a gun behind the display case and asks to see it. The clerk tells him it is a .22 Smith and Wesson. He says the gun will simply make the animal mad. The clerk tells Loomis if he wants to blow the animal's head off he needs a .357 Magnum. Loomis decides to go with the larger gun. Loomis is extremely impatient and tells the clerk to wrap the gun up. Mickey Dolenz is a musician/actor from the late 1960's. He was a member of The Monkees, a pop group. Mickey was cast as the crazy one on the show and if you have seen the show you know it is a perfect fit. Skyler plays the role of Tommy Doyal. Brad Douriff plays the role of Sheriff Brackett. Adam Weisman plays the role of Steve, Judith's boyfriend.

267.   Koplenson says, "He is out.".

Koplenson calls Loomis at home in the early morning hours to say that Michael has escaped. Koplenson tells Loomis that it is a massacre at the institution and Loomis says he is on the way. Loomis arrives at the institution and views the video of Michael's killing spree. Loomis yells at Koplenson and Morgan Walker, a hospital administrator. They try to place the blame on Loomis. They try to tell Loomis that if security was not enough he should have told them. Loomis jumps into his car, heading to Haddonfield to stop Michael.

Clint Howard plays the role of Dr. Koplenson. Clint plays a very inept Doctor in the movie. He doesn't seem to know if he is coming or going. Clint has played a great many roles, especially in his brother's movies. Clint is the brother of director/actor, Ron Howard. Udo Kier plays the role of Morgan Walker.

268.   Haddonfield Burger

Sheriff Brackett and Loomis are in the restaurant waiting for Loomis's order. Loomis tells Brackett that Michael has returned to Haddonfield. They both return to Brackett's office and talk further. Brackett asks Loomis why Michael has returned. Loomis tells Brackett to find her, meaning his baby sister. Brackett tells Loomis the story of how he found Laurie at Deborah's suicide scene.
He tells Loomis that his friends the Strodes adopted Laurie. Brackett calls the Strode's house and no one answers.

269.   Paul crashed his dad's motorcycle.

The girls all sit in the library studying. Annie is begging Laurie to watch Lindsay so she can go out with Paul. Lynda says, "I thought Paul was grounded for crashing his dad's motorcycle". Annie tells her he got out of it. Annie continues to beg Laurie, who finally agrees to watch Lindsay. Laurie looks at the window and Michael is outside staring in at her.

270.   WNKW

Taylor Madison, the reporter on the scene of the murders, is describing the incident. Taylor tells how the bodies were found. He says that Ronnie, Deborah's boyfriend, was found bound and stabbed 17 times. He reports that Steve, Judith's boyfriend was the victim of a deadly baseball bat beating.
He then reports the death of Judith Myers. He reports that 10 year old Michael Myers is the primary suspect.

271. **Daisy**

Joe Grizzly pulls his rig into the truck washing station to be cleaned. He tells the guys who work there to be careful with the rig. Joe just had the rig painted. Joe enters the bathroom and stops as he sees his reflection in the mirror. Joe fixes his hair before he goes into the bathroom stall. Michael enters the bathroom right after Joe. Joe sits down in the stall and starts to read a magazine. Joe first sees Michael's muddy feet. Michael knocks on the door to the stall. Joe tells him the stall is occupied and he will be a while. Michael knocks on the stall door again. Joe is angry now and pulls out a knife. Joe says, "You just hold on Daisy I got something for you". Joe opens the door and tells Michael his name is Big Joe Grizzly. Joe tells Michael he is going to cut that mask right off his face. Michael then rushes Joe and slams him into the backwall. Michael bangs Joe against the bathroom stall walls. Michael bangs Joe so hard against the walls that a glass case on the otherside of the wall breaks. Michael get the knife from Joe and stabs him with it. Michael kills Joe Grizzly. Michael puts on Joe's overalls and work boots. As Michael leaves the bathroom in his new attire, we see Joe lying dead on the floor in long underwear and socks. Michael of course has a mask covering his face as he walks away.

Ken Foree plays the role of Big Joe Grizzly. Joe seems to be a friendly and charming guy as evidenced by his demeanor at the truck stop. He even jokes with Michael when he knocks on the bathroom door. Ken has also been in "The Devil's Rejects". Ken is a native of Indiana, he was born there in 1948.

272. **eggs**

Cynthia is in the kitchen cooking breakfast. She is making scrambled eggs. Cynthia calls for Mason and Laurie to come eat breakfast. Mason comes into the kitchen and he looks confused. He tells Cynthia he can't find his glasses. Cynthia takes one look at Mason and hands him his glasses off the top of his head. Laurie comes into the kitchen right after Mason. Mason is reading the morning paper and eating half a bagel.

He is upset because the local hardware store is going out of business. Cynthia says good, because they have been ripping people off for 42 years. Laurie makes a crude joke about the owner of the store which upsets Cynthia.

She ask Laurie if she is going to eat and Laurie tells her she will get something at school. Cynthia sits down at the table by herself and eats her eggs.

273.   real estate

Laurie is walking out the door for school. Mason comes out behind her and tells her not to forget to drop the papers off at the Myers' house. We see Mason's car parked in front of the house with a Strode Realty sign on the side. She yells to him she won't forget. Mason tells her that he is trying to sell the house and it is very important. She reassures him again that she won't forget. Mason tells Laurie he loves her and Laurie says the same back. As Laurie is walking away Cynthia comes out of the house and tells Mason he forgot his briefcase. Laurie turns around and smiles as she sees her parents kissing. Laurie is walking towards the house when she is stopped by Tommy. Tommy is the boy Laurie babysits. Tommy asks Laurie why she is walking this walk to school.

She tells him she has to drop off some papers at the Myers' house. When Tommy and Laurie get to the Myer's house there is a empty real estate sign holder in the yard. Tommy tells Laurie that she isn't supposed to go up there. Laurie takes the papers out and puts them in the mail slot.

She messes with Tommy by acting like someone is pulling the mail from the other side. Little does she know Michael is on the other side of the door. He takes the papers and smells them. On the envelop as Michael puts it to his face we see a Strode Realty sticker on it. Laurie and Tommy walk away.

274.   Mother Teresa

Laurie, Linda, and Annie are sitting in the school's library supposedly studying. Annie is pleading with Laurie to watch Lindsey for her tonight. Annie wants to spend some time alone with Paul at the Wallace's house. The Wallace's are Lindsey's parents. Annie wants Laurie to pretend like she is watching Lindsey. Linda says she thought Paul was grounded and Annie says he got off. Laurie looks out the window while the other two are talking and sees Michael across the street. It looks like Michael is staring right at her. Annie continues to plead with Laurie. Laurie asks about what to do if the Wallaces come home and Annie says the mom is a lush and won't be home until late. Annie persists and Laurie tells her she doesn't like to lie. Annie asks, "God, what are you Mother Teresa?" Linda then grabs Laurie and says she is an angel. The girls all start to laugh at this. Laurie finally agrees to watch Lindsay. Annie tells her she loves her and Laurie says the same thing back. Laurie tells Annie she owes her for this.

Mother Teresa was a caretaker for the poor and suffering. She was born in 1910 and died in 1997. One thing I recall about her death is that Princess Diana died around the same time. Mother Teresa's death was overshadowed by Princess Di. I believe this wouldn't have bothered her because she lived for others and not herself.

275.   Michael snaps her neck.

Cynthia and Laurie are sitting on the front porch. They are handing out candy to little kids because it is Halloween night. Mason comes outside and sits down next to them. They talk for a few minutes before Annie arrives to pick up Laurie. The Strodes say hi to Annie and ask how her father is. Annie says, "Oh you know same as always". Cynthia asks Mason what that means and he say he has no idea . They both continue to smile at Annie. Laurie leaves with Annie to go babysitting. This is the last time Laurie sees her parents alive. Mason asks Cynthia if she is going to give him some loving. Cynthia tells him she will after they talk about the vacation. Cynthia goes into the house to stoke the fire in the fireplace. Mason is standing on the front porch finishing his cigarette when Michael appears and snatches him into the house. Michael shuts the front door violently. Mason is dead and Cynthia is staring dumbstruck at Michael. Michael assaults Cynthia and we see her crawl into another room. Michael picks up a picture of Laurie and Cynthia knocks it out of his hand.

She says, "Not my baby". Michael is holding her by her hair and she is on her knees.

Michael pulls her head back and snaps her neck. Sometime later on Sheriff Brackett calls the Strode house. The answering machine comes on and we hear a Halloween greeting. As the message plays we see the destruction Michael has caused and we see the Strode's bodies.

276.   Pookie

Laurie and Linda are walking out of school for the day. Linda tells Laurie she can't believe she is suspended from the squad. She says she doesn't mean to sound conceited, but she is the hottest cheerleader they have. Laurie laughs and says that doesn't sound conceited at all. Laurie asks Linda what happened to get her suspended. Linda tells Laurie the Coach gave them three new cheers to learn. Linda asked the Coach why they didn't do the cheers commando and then nobody would notice they were doing the same old cheers.

The Coach called Linda's dad and told him what Linda said. Laurie asks Linda what her dad said to this. Linda says, "Oh who cares". She will just tell him that Daddy's little pookie would never say anything like that. She tells Laurie she will give him the old suck up routine. Laurie says ever since your parents split up you have your father wrapped. Linda says, "Totally wrapped".

277.   He is stabbed.

Bob and Linda pull into the Myer's driveway. They both get out of the van and head into the house. Linda and Bob are both upset that the house is being sold. Bob tells Linda not to worry they will find another house to party in. Bob tells Linda he is going to fix up the van. The kids don't notice Michael standing on the upstairs veranda as they enter the house. Linda and Bob make love in Judith's old room. Linda tells Bob she wants another beer. Bob leaves the room to go get the beer from the van. As he walks down the hallway, we see a flash of Michael at the end of it. Bob goes down the steps and Michael follows him halfway and stops. Bob goes to the van and gets the beer. Linda is upstairs listening to the radio and waiting for Bob to return. Bob is walking towards the room when Michael attacks him. Bob struggles for a few seconds, but Michael gets the best of him. Michael picks Bob up by the throat and then jams a knife into him. The knife holds Bob up against the wall, off of the floor. Michael turns his head slightly as he looks at Bob's dead body. Michael then takes the sheet Bob was wearing and puts it on. Michael enters the room with Bob's sheet and glasses on. Linda laughs at Bob and tells him to give her the beer. He holds the beer out for her to get. Linda gets up and gets the beer. She turns her back to Michael and he grabs and chokes her.

This scene is almost identical to the death scene of Michael's sister Judith and her boyfriend, Steve. Steve leaves the room after making love to Judith. Judith turns on her headphones which are playing the song "Don't Fear the Reaper". This is the same song Linda listens to when Bob leaves the room. As Steve is walking towards the kitchen, we see a flash of Michael in the hallway. He follows Steve to the kitchen where he kills him. I think Michael is somehow associating Linda with his sister and is replaying her murder. Just my opinion, but I think it is right.

278.   Sid Haig

Dr. Loomis has asked the groundskeeper to take him to the Myer's grave site. They both get out of the car. Samuel has been trying to get in touch with Sheriff Brackett. His cell phone dies and he asks Chester if he can borrow his. Chester tells him he doesn't have one because it causes brain cancer. They walk towards the site and Chester tells Loomis he remembers the incident like it was yesterday. Chester says Deborah didn't like the label of Satan's mother so she killed herself. He says he thinks she shot herself in the head. He then says the doctor on the case wrote a book. Chester said it was blood money. Loomis replies, "Yeah I read that book it was a masterpiece". They get to where the grave is supposed to be and Chester has a fit. He says why do they do this sick crap. Loomis turns to walk away and Chester asks him where he is going. Loomis tells him he knows whose grave that is. The grave stone has been removed and there is a dead animal spread on a cross on the site.
Sid Haig plays the role of Chester Chesterfield. In the extras on the DVD it is explained how Sid got involved. Sid said he was sitting around his house when Rob called. Rob asked him if he would come and play the role of Chester Chesterfield.

Sid said they film his scene over the weekend. Sid has also played the role of Captain Spaulding in "House of 1000 Corpses" and "The Devil's Rejects". Rob Zombie is the director for the movie. In my opinion did an excellent job. It didn't feel like a remake, but an extension to the original. It has quickly become one of my favorite movies. Brad Dourif plays Sheriff Brackett. Clint Howard plays Dr. Koplenson.

279.   Dee Wallace Stone

Laurie is on her way from school when she sees her mom in the front yard. Laurie does not see Michael following her. Laurie asks her mom what she is doing. Her mom tells her she is putting Mr. Bones back together. Mr. Bones is a plastic skeleton that is used as a Halloween decoration. Cynthia puts one piece of him together and another falls off. She asks Laurie for some help. Cynthia tells Laurie she has been working on him for two hours. Laurie asks why she just doesn't throw it away. Cynthia says because Mason likes it. They finally fix Mr. Bones. As Cynthia and Laurie walk in the house, Cynthia tells Laurie she is still upset from that morning. She tells Laurie that the joke she told about the hardware store owner was inappropriate. She says there are some things a mom doesn't want to hear. Laurie tells her it is just a joke and they go into the house.

Dee Wallace Stone is, in my opinion, one of the best scream queens of all time. She has been in "Howling" where she played a woman who transformed into a werewolf. She has also starred in the original "The Hills Have Eyes". "The Hills Have Eyes" is my first quiz ever put online. In the movie, I think she is trying to be a cool mom. She seems to be a bit protective of Lori. Maybe that is because she knows Lori's secret. When Michael attacks her I get the feeling she knows it is Lori's brother. It is just the way she stares at him.

280.   Michael puts a pumpkin on his head.

Paul picks up Annie at the Doyle house. Annie and Paul then drive over to the Wallace house. Paul and Annis start to make out. In the background, we see Michael watching them. While Paul and Annie are kissing, we see Michael grab Paul and throw him to the floor. Michael kills Paul and then goes after Annie. Michael chases Annie through the house and into the kitchen, Annie grabs a knife, but Michael punches her and knocks her out. Annie wakes up and tries to get away, but Michael drags her back inside the house. Laurie is bringing Lindsey home from watching her. Lindsey turns on the lights in her house and starts to scream. Paul is hanging from the ceiling by a cord with a jack-o-lantern on his head. Laurie sees Annie lying on the floor and tells Lindsey to go get help. Laurie goes to call 911 and Michael, who is standing behind the door, closes it.

281.   Night of the Living Dead

Mr. Elrod was watching 'Night of the Living Dead', while Mrs. Elrod was making sandwiches.

282.   Ziggy

Jimmy tells Bud that his little brother Ziggy went to school with Laurie.

283.   WWAR

284.   Ben Tramer

This is the same boy who Laurie has a crush on.

285.   Robert Mundy

286.   Ford

This ambulance is quite old.

287.   Dementia

Mr. Garrett is watching tv when he should be watching the security monitors.

288.   The Keepsake

289.   Red

Karen gives Dorothy a ride after the Halloween party.

290.   eyes

291.   whole wheat

Annie was cooking egg whites for breakfast. Her dad was getting ready to leave for work. She told her dad not to forget to pick up the pizza for dinner. Annie told him to get a whole wheat crust pizza. Sheriff Brackett made a comment that he might as well get the pizza made out of cardboard. Laurie told Sheriff Brackett not to put any meat on the pizza.

Sheriff Brackett brought home a pizza with meat on one side and pineapple on the other. The family was sitting around the table enjoying a meal and talking. Laurie suddenly became ill and ran upstairs to the bathroom to vomit.

She was sharing some kind of mental link with Michael. Michael was eating a dog at the time and this was what made Laurie ill.

292. Frankenstein

Big Lou was the owner of the dance club that Deborah Myers had worked at. In one scene, we saw Big Lou dressed in the mask handing out candy to kids. He was also on the news and promoting his club. Big Lou put on the mask and was going to make love to his girlfriend, Misty, when Michael burst in the room. Lou pulled out a gun from his desk drawer and attempted to scare Michael. Michael killed Big Lou and then killed Misty.

I am not totally sure, but I believe this was revenge for Michael. The club advertised Deborah Myers as having worked there and being the mother of Michael. Michael also killed the bouncer of the club.

293. Magenta

Harley and Mya had a group theme for their costumes. They first asked Laurie to attend the Halloween party when they arrived to work their shift at the store. Laurie did not seem that keen on going to the party. Later on, after Laurie discovered that she was Michael's sister, she wanted to let loose. We saw the three girls walking in their costumes. They were all dressed as characters from "The Rocky Horror Picture Show". Mya was dressed as Columbia and Harley was dressed as Dr. Frank-N-Furter.

Laurie got extremely drunk at the party. Harley found a guy and went off to make out with him. Harley was in the guy's van as he went off to use the bathroom. Michael killed both the guy and Harley.

294.   Angel

Laurie was walking through town and she passed by a book store. In the window of the store was Dr. Loomis' book. Laurie started to walk by, but then decided to go in and get the book. She was reading the book in her car when she found out that she was adopted. She also found out that her name was Angel Myers. This was news to Laurie because her parents never informed her she was adopted.

Sheriff Brackett also read the book and got extremely upset with Dr. Loomis. In the previous film, Brackett told Loomis of the story of Laurie. Brackett told Loomis that he made a promise to Laurie's parents never to let anyone know the circumstances behind the Strodes getting Laurie.

295.   Uncle Meat's Java Hole

Laurie pulled up for work in her car. As Laurie got out of the car, we saw the sign for the store. The store was owned by a certified hippie named Uncle Meat. Meat made a comment to Laurie that she was late. Laurie then explained to Meat that she had worked overtime the previous night. Meat told Laurie she needed to loosen up. Laurie asked Meat if that meant she could come to work when she wanted to. Meat told Laurie not on his dime. Meat then went off on a tangent about how corporate America sucked. It was obvious Laurie and Mya, Meat's other employee, were paying him no attention. Uncle Meat walked back to his office feeling dejected. Howard Hesseman played the role of Uncle Meat. Howard is probably better known for his television work; he played Dr. Johnny Fever on "WKRP in Cincinnati". He also played Charles P. 'Charlie' Moore on the sitcom "Head of the Class".

296.   white horse

This horse was to be a significant component of the movie. It was how we saw Deborah throughout the entire movie. She was most of the time standing with the horse. Michael first saw her with the horse under a streetlight on a dark country road. This was where Deborah informed Michael of what he had to accomplish to get his family back together.

The horse was significant because it was the last thing Deborah gave Michael before she died. We saw Michael and Deborah sitting at a table talking. Michael was still in the hospital for the crimes he committed. Michael' mom gave him the white toy horse as a gift. She asked him if he liked it and he said that he did. The reason we saw Deborah with the horse is because this is how Michael remembered her.

297.   They thought he was homeless and stealing from them.

In this scene, we saw the two men and a woman in a truck driving through a field looking for Michael. They had warned him not to trespass on their property previously. They found Michael and the two men got out of the truck and beat him. The woman told the men to stop, as she was afraid they were going to kill him. The men returned to the truck and the woman stayed by Michael's side. She apologized to Michael for the beating he had just endured. The men and woman were getting back into the truck when Michael got up. Up to this point in the movie he did not have his mask on.

He put on the mask and then killed the two men, the woman, and their dog.

298.   Lynda's dad

Dr. Loomis was in the bookstore signing his latest book. Kyle van der Klok stepped up to where Loomis was seated. He handed Loomis his book and inside was a photo. Loomis asked Kyle if he wanted him to sign the picture. Kyle asked him if he recognized the girl and Loomis said no. Kyle told Lomis it was his daughter, Lynda, and that Loomis was responsible for her death. Loomis tried to apologize to Kyle, but Kyle pulled out a gun to shoot Loomis.

The security at the store apprehended Kyle and took him away.

It was later revealed the gun was not even loaded.

299.   Annie was getting ready to brush her teeth.

Annie was in the bathroom preparing to brush her teeth. Michael was standing in the hallway watching her. Annie had not noticed Michael yet. She was going about her routine when she looked up and saw Michael standing there. Annie slammed the door to prevent Michael from getting her. Annie tried to run away from Michael.

Sadly, Michael caught and killed Annie.

This was the saddest moment in the film for me. Annie had already been through and survived one attack by Michael. She was trying to work past all of the emotional and physical damage Michael had caused her. Laurie had come home to find Annie lying in the bathroom barely alive. She kept telling Annie to stay with her, but Annie was telling Laurie to run. Annie died in Laurie's arms.

Danielle Harris played the role of Annie. She is a veteran of the series, having played Jamie Lloyd in "Halloween 4" and "Halloween 5".

300. **Nobody**

Dr. Loomis wanted to make things right and help Sheriff Brackett out. He ran into the shack were Laurie was with Michael. She was screaming at Loomis to help her. She told Loomis she was being held and Loomis looked at her. There was nobody there and Loomis tried to tell Laurie that.

He told her it was all in her mind. Michael approached Loomis and killed him. In this scene, we heard the adult Michael speak for the first time. He said, "Die".

Made in the USA
Columbia, SC
26 September 2024

43132994R00061